PARADISE LOST
The Decline of the
Auto-Industrial Age

PARADISE LOST
The Decline of the Auto-Industrial Age

EMMA ROTHSCHILD

RANDOM HOUSE  *NEW YORK*

Library of Congress Cataloging in Publication Data.
Rothschild, Emma, 1948–
Paradise lost.
1. Automobile industry and trade—United States.
I. Title.
HD9710.U52R66   338.4′7′6292220973   73-3984
ISBN 0-394-46032-4

Manufactured in the United States of America

First Edition

To my parents

"When I grew up in New Jersey, the automobile was the one product that universally signified success in America. What has happened on the way to Paradise?"

Ed Mullane, president of the Ford Dealers' Alliance, in *Automotive News*, May 1970

"Paradise Lost: Utopian GM Plant in Ohio Falls From Grace Under Strain of Balky Machinery, Workers."

Headline for an article about GM's Lordstown factory, in the *Wall Street Journal*, January, 1972

Contents

PARADISE LOST
The Decline of the
Auto-Industrial Age

1

Automotive Troubles

The auto industry finds troubles, every way it turns. The expansion of auto sales and profits in the national boom of 1971 to 1973 has failed to improve the industry's prospects. Its past assurance is lost in new and unpredictable problems. Demoralization is expressed by the highest executives of auto corporations and dealers' associations, by industry financial analysts. A few billion dollars of annual profit can no longer satisfy auto expectations: automotive profits have skidded upwards and downwards for the last ten years, yet even the good years cannot reassure the industry. $2.7 billion may not seem meager as the 1971 profit of the four U.S. automakers, but for the *Wall Street Journal*, that year, Detroit's profit-making "formula just doesn't seem to have the old magic." The chairman of General Motors, Richard Gerstenberg, felt it necessary in December 1971 to remind national audiences of the "serious lack of understanding about the need for profits in the American economy"; his predecessor, James Roche, said, modestly, at the end of 1971, a year in which GM made a profit after tax of $1.9 billion, that "profits have not been as good as I would like to have seen them."

When GM early in 1973 reported record sales and production, and the largest annual profit ever made by any company anywhere, corporation executives seemed less than grateful. GM's chairman and president noted a "lower profit margin compared with 1965 in a year of record sales," mentioning corporate efforts at "continued cost-reduction," and the "adverse effects of local strikes"; the corporation's good news failed to stimulate the depressed Wall Street price of GM shares for more than a few days. Such caution was surprisingly reasonable. GM's total profit amounted to $2.16 billion—but the profit it made for every vehicle it produced, in real terms, adjusted for inflation in the value of money, was actually lower than it had been in 1965, or in 1955, or in 1950, or in 1928. If the company had in 1972 made as much profit, in real terms, for every vehicle as it made in 1928, its total profits would have been some $800 million higher.

Automotive executives have reacted to their new troubles with mystified and defensive disbelief. A president of the National Auto Dealers' Association has called for resistance in the face of peril: "I think it is high time that teamwork spread through the industry—our own, to the parts industry, the oil industry and so on." For Roche of GM, the present American consumer movement constitutes "a form of harassment unknown to businessmen in other times." For *Automotive News*, the "Newspaper of the Industry," and the auto dealers' trade journal, "The automobile industry is suffering the slings and arrows of outrageous fortune to a greater degree today than at any time in its history"; there is every week "a new attack aimed at the auto business. There is no segment of this business that is not affected and there seems to be no let up in sight." GM's director of advertising tells the National Auto Auction Association that American business, and in particular the auto industry, is being "painted by a broad brush of distortion." For Ed Mullane, head of the insurgent Ford Dealers' Alliance, times are even more melancholy: "When I grew up in New Jersey," he says, "the automobile was the one product that universally signified success in America. What has happened on the way to Paradise?"

The auto industry's troubles are now so well known that one international auto corporation, Fiat, has even tried to use them to sell cars. Recent Fiat advertisements summarize the industry's problems, its sense of being besieged on all fronts. One explains that "In recent years, the car has come in for a lot of criticism. And rightfully so. It creates pollution. It creates congestion. It creates accidents. It's growing bigger, and more powerful, and more expensive than it has to be. . . ." (So, rush out and buy a small Fiat, although another Fiat advertisement published at the same time proclaims that "Everyone likes big cars.") A second Fiat advertisement, published in France, provides a short history of automotive culture: "In the thirties and forties, in the U.S., the automobile began to change. Instead of remaining a practical and efficient means of transportation, it became a symbol of wealth and power.... Our cities are [now] jammed by traffic. The number of deaths and accidents increases each year," and cities are also, according to the advertisement, troubled by parking problems and auto-motive pollution.

The importers of Swedish Saab cars boast that "Bored people build bad cars. That's why we're doing away with the assembly line." American oil corporations have followed Fiat's lead. A recent advertisement by the Atlantic Richfield Company shows a (black-and-white) photograph of a snaking, stalled traffic jam, and a green-and-red-checkered abstract painting. The painting is "The ideal," and the traffic jam "The real." "The real": "Our cities have been tied up in stifling automotive congestion because we have emphasized cars at the expense of other means of transportation" (and because we are "blinded" by "our love for the automobile"). "The ideal": "We will build diversified, balanced, transportation networks. . . ."

An Unpopular Marriage

The most public of the auto industry's troubles, and the one which most alarms the industry, is its trouble with the car-buying public. More than 9 million people bought new American cars in 1972; yet early in 1973, Lee A. Iacocca, the president of Ford, chose to emphasize corporate fears, proclaiming that the auto industry "has been backed to the cliff edge of desperation" by federal antipollution regulations. American Motors, in March 1973, announced a "long-term goal" of diversification, and reduction of the passenger-car part of its business to as little as half of its total activities.

Sales of American cars are growing unreliably, and the

car seems, as Ed Mullane discerns, an increasingly unpopular commodity. The industry's explanations for this depression range from the fatalistic—a Ford vice-president has said that "more and more people view the automobile as an unfortunate necessity"—to the psychosexual, as in Roche of GM's famous pronouncement that "America's romance with the automobile is not over. Instead, it has blossomed into a marriage." Meanwhile cars, and the selling of cars, have become a national example of business irrationality. The chairman of a House Commerce subcommittee describes American automobiles as "overornamented," "overchromed," and overly expensive; the Federal Trade Commission demanded recently that various auto corporations document claims made in their advertisements, and it published the result—GM's explanation, for example, of its claim that the Chevrolet Chevelle has "109 advantages to keep it from becoming old before its time," mentioned such "advantages" as "a full line of models," a "classically simple new grille," "balanced wheels and tires," and a "body by Fisher."

More and more dealers and auto companies are resorting, like Fiat, to attacks on automotive pretensions, as a method of auto salesmanship. Honda advertises its sub-mini urban cars as status symbols in the automotive anticulture, the counter-automobile culture. The only auto dealer whose recent marketing techniques have attracted the sort of national attention auto dealers used to expect is a Seattle Chevrolet and Fiat dealer called Dick Balch: Mr. Balch's sales gimmick—which indicates some mysterious perception of automotive discontent—consists of showing television commercials in which he uses a twelve-pound sledgehammer to bash in the windshields, headlights, and fenders of his new cars; repairs cost him about $30,000 a year, but customers are eager to buy the bashed-in, repaired Chevrolets as new cars, and sales and profits are soaring at the Balch dealership.

The Rising Tide of Consumerism

The auto industry is also notably troubled by what *Automotive News* calls the "Rising Tide of Consumerism." The most famous success of the American consumer movement, and of Ralph Nader, has been its attack on the safety and pollution records of American cars. A former GM vice-president, and head of Chevrolet, J. Z. DeLorean, bleakly summarizes his worries on this score: the three most serious threats to the auto industry today are safety, ecology, and consumerism. *Motor Trend* magazine, once devoted to all-out auto enthusiasm, and recently merged with *Sports Car Graphic,* has now hired a Consumer Affairs editor, who addresses himself to such previously unimaginable topics as the (small, unpolluting) "Future of the Automobile in America," and "Twenty Auto Defects that could kill you."

Counting automotive dangers has become a major national enterprise. More than 30 million cars and trucks have been recalled since 1966 for the correction of safety defects. GM has adjusted the engine mounts on no fewer than six and a half million of its full-size Chevrolets; both the Ford Pinto and the Chevrolet Vega, Detroit's high-quality answers to foreign competition, were involved in safety recalls early in their careers, and Vegas alone have suffered three recalls. Auto corporations may now try to make a profit out of the necessity for building safer and less noxious cars, and Detroit executives already seem proud about the number of cars they recall each year; but the result so far of the consumer movement's assault on American cars has been to damage the auto corporations, both economically and in their reputation among consumers. (After GM and Ford were indicted in 1972 on a charge of fixing the prices of fleet cars, the U.S. government released copies of numerous internal company memoranda used in preparing the indictment. As summarized in the *Wall Street Journal*, one, puzzling, memorandum concerned a "wide-ranging conversation, duly reported" between the head of Chevrolet and Mr. Zollie Frank, "a major Chicago area auto dealer and a legendary entrepreneur": "Mr. Frank said none of his son's classmates would go to work for GM because of its reputation for stifling the individual and fouling the air. A certain tailgate window should go all the way up when the door is operated, Mr. Frank said.")

Dying Automobiles

Environmental criticism is another preoccupation of beleaguered automotive executives. The industry complains, justifiably, that the automobile has been made an international symbol of ecological destruction. No panorama of urban degradation is complete without a representation of dying automobiles piled in a deserted scrap yard. Automobiles are attacked as the major offenders in causing air pollution and wasting world energy resources, and for using the energy they consume increasingly inefficiently. The *Wall Street Journal*, in an editorial called "The Concrete Bloc," argues that the role of the automobile "will have to be smaller," that "urban concentrations of population bring about less need for and less economic advantage in the ownership of cars. Moreover, private cars contribute very seriously to the tensions and stress of crowded urban life. . . ." A study of energy conservation prepared for the Office of Emergency Preparedness says that "projected growth patterns" "in automobile consumption . . . seem unacceptable given present concern over the environment, world fuel reserves, and required U.S. dependence on foreign petroleum": "Automobiles account for much more than half of total transportation energy. Of the energy consumed by automobiles, 55 percent is consumed within urban areas, and 30 percent is consumed making trips of about ten miles or less. . . . The average low occupancy of commuter cars and the short distances travelled combine with traffic congestion to lower drastically the energy efficiency of the automobile."

Toyotas on the Beaches

Another of the auto industry's loudest laments concerns the Menace of Foreign Competition. At least until the introduction in August 1971 of Nixon's New Economic Policy (Nixon at the time explained the devaluation of the dollar in terms of its adverse effect on people who wanted to buy foreign cars), automobiles seemed to be, with transistor radios, shoes, and small calculating machines, the American commodities most threatened by foreign advances. The market penetration of imported cars—Toyotas on the beaches of Santa Monica—became the most frightening symptom for protectionist business of foreign competition and national depression. All the major U.S. automotive companies issued hortatory and often chauvinistic warnings against what one Ford executive described as a "significant negative attitude—a pro-foreign, anti-Detroit syndrome." The auto corporations tried at first to explain that foreign successes, particularly successes in making cheap cars, were a consequence of the docility of underpaid foreign workers; they now concede that their German and Japanese competitors build auto factories which are at least as advanced technologically as U.S. plants. Meanwhile, through their overseas operations, the U.S. companies are in bitter competition with foreign firms. The world auto market is only slightly more encouraging than the U.S. market, and many foreign auto makers, facing automotive saturation in their own domestic markets, are even more troubled than GM, Ford, and Chrysler; GM, which unlike Volkswagen has yet to suffer the indignity of a purge of top executives, has said that it expects its business in Europe and the underdeveloped world to expand faster than its U.S. operations, with Latin America and Southeast Asia as particularly exciting prospects.

Insurance, Parking, Repairs

Everyone who has to support an automobile knows about automotive inflation. Insurance costs, parking costs, maintenance costs, dealer costs, spare-parts costs, repair costs, have all multiplied: average Americans spend a tenth of their incomes on automotive transportation, and the cost of operating a car is increasing faster than the cost of living. These increases in the total cost of motoring are beginning to hurt the auto corporations, not least by creating dissension among the many industries that serve the American automobile. Auto insurance corporations were prominent in early attacks on Detroit for building dangerous, overpowered cars that were expensive to repair, and seemed to delight in smashing new model cars to prove their frailty. Auto repair companies have sued the auto insurers for coercion and price conspiracy. Congress tries to impose federal controls on auto repairing. An auto-components executive pronounces that automobiles have been replaced as status symbols by "snowmobiles, trail bikes, boats, trailer homes, and the like." Other parts companies complain about the inflated cost of auto parts produced "in-house" by the four auto makers. Even American auto dealers, once the most devoted servants of the auto corporations, are now restive. Many dealers are in serious economic trouble; dissident dealer groups, like Mr. Mullane's, are among the auto makers' most effective critics, and other dealers even pass information to the Center for Auto Safety, which is associated with Ralph Nader. One of *Fortune* magazine's automotive experts, discussing auto dealers' problems, describes corporate boasts about improved auto service as "spewing forth clouds of puffery."

Three Pigs (Who Lived in Detroit)

Another indication of the auto industry's troubles—of a different sort—is the extent to which many sections of

American business opinion have turned against the auto corporations. One sign of the times, from a 1972 front page of the *Wall Street Journal*, was an article beginning: "Once upon a time there were three pigs (who lived in Detroit) during the reign of good King Richard. (Now this is a fable, so don't confuse the pigs with anything nasty. These pigs are the nice, clean-toed, storybook kind. . . .) " GM, Ford, and Chrysler as clean-toed pigs? The article, which would have been blasphemous five years earlier, was an allegory about the auto industry and Phase II of Nixon's economic policy. It went on to describe how the pigs, despite price guide-lines, grew very fast, how the biggest one, "General Pig," swelled, how the "Wolf" (Price) Commission suspected that it "had been tricked," how the pig's greed continued. . . . At a more practical level, Wall Street disdain had seriously damaged the position of auto-corporation stocks on the New York Stock Exchange. As one Ford executive put it, in testimony before the Price Commission, "It is clear that the financial community is becoming unenthusiastic about the investment outlook for the automotive industry and for Ford." Even when auto profits have been high, auto-share prices have often remained depressed Brokers' recommendations have failed to persuade institutional and private investors to hold "undervalued" auto stocks; a Wall Street share analyst told *The New York Times* early in 1973 that "The big thing now is investor psychology [and] nobody wants the autos"; a 1972 column in *Forbes* business magazine advised readers to buy municipal bonds or leave their money on bank deposit, because growth stocks were risky, "And who wants the nongrowth or slow growth stocks like GM?"

Obsolescent Processes

An even more serious problem for the auto companies, recognized by business opinion and by auto executives themselves, is that automotive technology is no longer a growth area of American industrial engineering. Edward Cole, president of GM, admits that the "possibility of further technological improvement in our business is not as great as in the past. . . . You can't" (for financial reasons, apparently) "just go in and tear up plants. . . ." Other auto industrialists say that foreign auto companies are sometimes more advanced technologically than American firms. The only major postwar automotive advance applied seriously by the U.S. auto industry is the Wankel rotary engine—a German invention, first developed efficiently in Japan, and studied in America by a GM division which specialized in aerospace work. A U.S. government study describes the auto industry as "an often mentioned example" of a business on the borderline between the dynamic, internationally competitive group of "technology-intensive" industries, and the old-fashioned, depressed group of "non-technology-intensive" industries. Where, in the 1920s, 1930s, and 1940s, the auto industry was a model of American productive superiority, the industry now appears technologically less glamorous than electronics, computer, antipollution industries: a GM advertisement published as long ago as the early 1960s shows a blue Cadillac parked in front of a sign saying "Electronics Laboratories." Industry executives themselves proclaim— as an argument against union wage demands—that the growth of automotive productivity is disastrously and unprecedentedly low. *Fortune* magazine, a notable partisan of high-technology industries, has speculated whether GM's rate of return on capital is in a situation of long-term decline; it calls elsewhere for new technologies "to restructure our older industries, which are now the major offenders against the environment because their own processes are rapidly growing obsolescent. The wheel-on-steel railroad dates basically from 1800; the steam power plant, based on the Carnot cycle, from 1824; the automobile, based on the 4-cycle Otto engine, from 1876," and concludes that "the [auto] industry's general technological capabilities have raised a lot of questions lately."

Detroit

Another public sign of automotive distress is the decline of Detroit as an industrial center. Downtown Detroit has become a national monument to the dilapidation of the central city and the troubles of urban industry. Unemployment in Detroit and in Michigan is well above the national average. Nixon's 1971 removal of the auto excise tax was expressly designed to stimulate employment, but automotive hiring increased much less fast than auto sales and profits. The auto corporations participate in schemes to rehabilitate the downtown area of Detroit, but they expand their own operations fastest in rural and suburban Michigan, in Ohio, in the South—as GM plans to do in Jackson, Mississippi, or did when it built its expensive new Vega factories at Lordstown, Ohio, in a depressed area of poor farmland and declining steel mills. Month after month, auto-components firms close their Detroit factories. Even a bankers' adver-

tisement for the State of Michigan repudiates the auto business: "Some people have the strange notion that Michigan's
growth is limited by a dependence on the auto industry,"
but Michigan is also, for example, a center for "tourism
and recreation," "in fact, more than 67 percent of our
workers have nonmanufacturing jobs."

The Primacy of Man in the Balance Sheet

At least since 1936, when Charles Chaplin was inspired by
a newspaper reporter's horrified stories about Detroit to
make *Modern Times*, auto-assembly factories have stood
for all that is intolerable in modern industrial work. Yet the
discontent of contemporary auto workers is one of the most
famous manifestations of present automotive troubles (and
for the auto corporations, a most notable tribulation). Business commentators who discover the "blue collar revolt"
generally use the attitudes of auto assembly workers as an
illustration of the alienation of the modern spirit. *Fortune*,
in an article called "Blue Collar Blues," describes the "un-
derstanding gap" ("curiously reminiscent of the gaps
between parents and children and between universities and
students") between management and workers in the auto
industry, and argues that auto industry managers cannot
appreciate workers' "frail contemporary psyches." Every
angry movement of American labor is found in the auto
industry. Militant organizations of black industrial workers
have been most powerful in Detroit auto factories. White
working-class radical support for George Wallace, in the
1968 and 1972 election years, was prominent in auto fac-

tories, particularly in the rural north and south of Michigan. The discontent of young, "independent-minded" production workers is widespread in auto factories from New Jersey to California to Ohio: the 1972 strike over working conditions by young workers at GM's Lordstown factories is the most famous contemporary example of worker alienation. At the time of that strike, even business opinion came close to criticizing GM for a lack of humanity in its plant management: for *Business Week* the "spreading Lordstown syndrome" called attention to the "increasingly serious problem of worker discontent on automated assembly lines everywhere"; *The New York Times* described the strike editorially as a rebellion against the "dehumanizing effect of automation," against employee frustrations which "differ only in intensity from those expressed in *Modern Times*," and against "the empty, repetitive nature of [assembly line] duties," and it called for a restoration of the "primacy of man" in the "balance sheet"; even the *Wall Street Journal* commented editorially that in the Lordstown dispute it found itself uncharacteristically neutral as between management and labor, since the "real culprit" was "assembly line monotony," and the issues involved were "far deeper than they seem."

A Host of Environmental Problems

Of all automotive troubles, perhaps the most intractable, and certainly for the auto industry the bitterest and least expected, is the "social" or "sociological" attack on automotive development. Henry Ford II described this assault in a speech given during the Transpo '72 Exposition in Washington: "The automobile industry and the so-called highway lobby have been blamed for causing a host of environmental problems—including, to name just a few, air, noise, and visual pollution, urban traffic congestion, unplanned suburban sprawl, the decay of central cities, the decline of public transportation and the segregation of minorities in urban ghettoes." Mass, off-highway, nonautomobile transportation is now acclaimed as an American growth industry, with important potential for advances in technology and productivity. Transportation accounts for 20 percent of the U.S. Gross National Product, of which 83 percent is spent on highway, auto, and truck transport. Yet the auto industry has itself conceded recently that motor taxes can be used for purposes other than building highways: Henry Ford, high GM executives, the National Auto Dealers' Association, and the chairman of the world's largest gasoline corporation, Standard Oil of New Jersey, or Exxon, now agree that some small part of the Highway Trust Fund may be diverted to urban and interurban mass transit. (The Highway Trust Fund, established in 1956, reserved revenues from gasoline taxes for highway construction.) Auto manufacturers describe themselves as total transportation organizations (just as oil companies say that they are in the total energy business), although the auto industry's real attitude to transportation planning remains ambivalent. Auto executives continue to describe the future of American transportation as a pageant of big and little cars, electric and gasoline-powered, urban and suburban, on-highway and off-highway, remote-controlled and owner-operated. A Ford executive, identified as the "concepts manager" for Ford

Car Research, expresses this vision of travel to come: roads will be built on two or three levels of office buildings, commuters will drive small urban cars, which will serve as "small security vaults" against the criminality of the central city; cars will be loaded for vacation travel, 350 at a time, onto a "car jumbo jet" version of C5A military transport planes. The industry's long-term perspective, in the face of a national attack on the social consequences of automotive development, has been well summarized by one of the industry's academic friends: "Transportation *is* social progress," writes the author of *The Road and the Car in American Life*, a study assisted by the Automobile Manufacturers' Association, and "there is no substitute in sight for the highway and the motorized vehicle."

In this book, I will look at the different troubles afflicting the auto business, and at the connections among them. For the auto industry itself, the troubles described above seem mysterious and distinct. Industry spokesmen sometimes imply that it is a temporary quirk of fate, or of American mass psychology, that U.S. auto makers should simultaneously be harassed by consumers, threatened by foreigners, patronized by business commentators, persecuted by their employees, sickened with economic and technological lethargy. Yet it seems unlikely that these different misfortunes can have fallen from the sky above Detroit. What I want to attempt here is to look for a more convincing relationship among various automotive anxieties, for a relationship that is true to the political and economic reality of the auto industry's present situation.

Such an explanation must take account of the auto industry's past troubles and past successes, and also of the
experience of other, comparable industries; a starting place
might be the early development of the auto corporations in
Detroit. One candid view of world auto history has been
proposed, surprisingly enough, by an international auto in-
dustrialist, Giovanni Agnelli of Fiat. All international auto
corporations, he argues, now face serious problems of
consumer demand and efficient production. Each national
industry has experienced a period of dramatic growth, when
sales, production, and productivity expanded together—
after that period sales and profits fluctuate widely. In Japan,
according to Agnelli, auto production increased fast in the
1960s, in Western Europe in the 1950s, and in America
"the car boom flourished between the end of the First World
War and the Great Depression." The auto industry's problems follow from this historical situation.

During its period of rapid expansion, the U.S. auto industry experienced simultaneous successes in all the areas
where it is now troubled. Between 1918 and 1928, and to a
slightly lesser extent in the 1930s, American car sales increased dramatically; cars were the most glamorous of all
commodities, and "universally signified success in America";
auto dealers were heroes, and the color, styling, engineering,
and appurtenances of new cars were a matter of national
preoccupation; U.S. manufacturers led the world in everything to do with the automobile business, including export
sales; Detroit was the pride of industrial America, where
prosperous auto workers were occasionally lucky enough to
be able to drive to work; auto factories, with their minutely
coordinated assembly lines, were the highest achievement of

modern manufacturing technology; Ford's Detroit factories attracted millions of amazed or admiring visitors, from the Italian car designer Pininfarina, to L.-F. Céline, to the Mexican socialist painter Diego Rivera, whose murals in the Detroit Art Institute commemorate the horrors, but also the power and the productiveness, of the Ford River Rouge plant; the auto industry led U.S. business in productivity growth during the unsurpassed economic boom of the 1920s; the jobs of auto workers were brutal and inhuman, yet the early auto corporations managed to deflect the discontent of many automobile workers, by their wages policy and (at least at Ford's, with its compulsory "Americanization" classes for the many foreign workers) by encouraging workers to feel a part of the greatest industrial machine in the history of the world, producing the most desirable commodity in America.

These successes of the glorious automotive past seem to suggest that the industry's present troubles might also add up to a metamorphosis in automotive fortunes. The auto corporations, with their dealers and suppliers and captive cities, may now, it seems, be experiencing, if not a long decline, at least a historical crisis from which the companies (and the cities) might emerge transformed. Business history is made up of the rise and fall of industries, of the lives of different businesses from youth to maturity to decrepitude; it seems that the modern auto business may be an example of a mature American industry, facing decline. *Fortune* compares "obsolescent" automobile technology with the technology of railroads: the railroad industry led the American industrial expansion of the second half of the nineteenth century, supported generations of American millionaires, and formed the geographical and productive development of the national economy; in the last few decades the railroad business has suffered a continuous decline, throwing millions of workers out of their jobs, destroying cities, bankrupting corporations and entrepreneurs. Any future successful railroads will be operated with new capital, new technologies, and a different (much reduced) work force, by new owners and for the benefit of different consumers. Other international businesses experienced similar fates. The late-nineteenth-century decline of the British railroad industry, simultaneously financial, social, political, psychological, has perhaps the most ominous similarity to the troubles of the U.S. auto business. The British textile industry, to take another example, supported and made possible British world economic leadership in the mid-nineteenth century; by the end of the century, threatened by foreign competition, attacked by progressive business opinion, and unable or unwilling to build new, advanced factories, the industry was expanding only in the farthest parts of the British Empire, and Manchester was an area of national distress.

This book will ask to what extent the many crises of the modern U.S. auto industry are connected, and to what extent they jointly constitute a historical decline in the industry's business life. The auto industry has had at least as much power over national development as the nineteenth-century railroad business in America or in Britain: through the growth of trucking and personal highway travel it has inflected economic and geographical development; through the growth of mass car ownership and suburban land-use planning it has affected the most intimate course of American social life; the industry's strength has been supported by an unprecedentedly powerful coalition of political forces. A decline in the automotive economy—not necessarily a catastrophe but even a modest weakening— would have the most serious consequences for the national economy and for national life, not only for the 25,000 American auto dealers and the 700,000 auto workers and the 1.5 million people who live in Detroit, but also for the entire social face of America.

I intend to look first at the economic situation of the auto corporations, at the past and present course of profits and sales and productivity, and at the ways in which automotive strategy is determined by Henry Ford's early theories of mass production, or "Fordism," and by the principles of elaborate and expensive selling established in the 1920s by Alfred Sloan of GM, which I will call "Sloanism." I will use General Motors as my main example of both effects— because it is the largest and least vulnerable of the four U.S. auto makers, and the largest manufacturing company in the world, and also because its secretiveness and toughness and single-mindedness make it peculiarly interesting.

I will then look at the American auto market, at American auto production, and at the extent to which they are affected by the troubles outlined above. Here again I will take GM's operations as a representative example: specifically, the market for GM's Vega car, and the production of the Vega at Lordstown, Ohio. The Vega was designed by GM as a small second car to help prevent the stagnation and saturation of the domestic car market, and to compete with such imported cars as the Toyota and the Volkswagen. It is sold as a simple, high-quality car, yet Vegas were recalled for safety defects three times in their first two years, and the car is attacked bitterly by the American consumer movement. The Vega factories suffer from as many of the auto industry's production troubles as the selling of the Vega suffers in marketing. The Lordstown plant was built by GM hastily, and at great expense, as a showplace for the corporation's most advanced technology. Vegas are assembled very fast, with much automation and with the help of twenty-six robots: GM has said that in building the Vega at Lordstown it wanted to show that an all-American car could be competitive in price and quality with foreign imports. The story of Lordstown is as notorious as the story of the Vega safety recalls: the Lordstown factory was built in a depressed rural area (according to *The New York Times* editorial quoted above, at "a location in the conservative heartland of America"), where most workers were white and young, were forced to commute as much as fifty or a hundred miles to work, and were new to union organization. But almost from the earliest days workers rebelled against plant management, and in the second year of the factory's operations the local union held its famous strike against GM, over plant working conditions. The Lordstown experience seems a representative, if extreme, example of the auto industry's problems with productivity and with its employees. I visited Lordstown several times, while the factory was being built and after the strike, and I will report the operations of GM's most advanced technology as it is seen by some of the people who work with it.

Returning to the more general situation of the auto industry, I will look next at the remarkable similarities between automotive problems and the problems of certain late-nineteenth-century British industries, and at some of the alternative courses now available to the U.S. auto corporations, as their domestic sales and production become more troublesome. One development is diversification, into such "para-automotive" markets as the recreational vehicle and mass-transportation businesses. Another is foreign expansion: particularly into underdeveloped (including Southeast Asian) countries, to which the advanced world industry is now trying to export its auto-dominated pattern of social development; and towards the international production of components for American cars, such as Ford's foreign-engined Pinto.

I will finish by asking to what extent the troubles shown may add up to an industrial decline, and to what extent the present power of auto corporations, components companies, auto dealers, motel owners, highway construction companies, of the highway lobby and of suburban real estate developers—of the auto-industrial complex—is no more than a temporarily dominant but mortal mutation of economic evolution.

2

Fordism and Sloanism

Some difficulties in the automotive economy are apparent from the simplest auto statistics.

————In the last fifty-five years, the world market for American cars has grown increasingly slowly. Expansion was most spectacular in the 1920s, when the automobile population of America grew more than seven times as fast as the human population. In 1920 there was one passenger car registered for every 13 Americans, and in 1930 there was one for every 5½ Americans. By the Great Depression, the United States had achieved a level of auto-motive saturation—of cars per man, woman, and child—that Britain, for example, reached in 1966, and Holland in 1970. Since the Second World War auto registrations have grown much more slowly: there was one car for every 3¾ Americans in 1950, one for every 3 Americans in 1960, and one for every 2¼ Americans in 1970. The only places, by 1970, which came fairly near to the United States in density of cars were the Principality of Monaco, the U.S. Virgin Islands, and, if military vehicles are counted as passenger cars, the Panama Canal Zone.

————While U.S. production faced a saturated home market, world auto production increased rapidly. In 1955 the United States produced 72 percent of all passenger cars made in the world; in 1959, 52 percent, and in 1969, 36 percent.

————After the Second World War, U.S. car sales fluctuated dizzily with booms and recessions in the national economy. From 1919 to 1949, the number of cars and trucks produced each year in America increased more than two and a half times, and General Motors' annual production increased almost six times. 1941 was the last year of peacetime production. In 1948 U.S. vehicle production passed its prewar level. From 1949 to 1971 U.S. car and truck production increased by less than three quarters, and GM's U.S. production barely doubled, in eleven huge leaps and falls. 1971 was a record year for auto sales in the United States, with 8.6 million cars produced, yet U.S. makers sold fewer cars per head of the population than they had in 1950, and barely more than in 1929.

————Even sales of auto improvements and optional accessories began to slow down in the late 1960s. By 1970, the market for many auto options was approaching saturation: 91 percent of all cars sold in America were equipped with automatic transmission, 85 percent with power steering, and 60 percent with air conditioning.

————The auto industry's troubles were reflected in the growth of dollar profits. 1971 was a year of national economic upturn, when the auto market was stimulated in the spring by the industry's recovery from the 1970 GM strike, and in the fall by the removal of the 7 percent auto excise tax. Yet the auto manufacturers' real profits (adjusted for changes in the value of money) were lower than they had been in 1966, 1965, 1964, or 1955. The rate of profit on invested capital was similarly disappointing, and companies making autos and auto parts earned a lower profit on stockholders' equity than the average for all corporations in the *Fortune* 500 directory. Dollar profits were at an all-time record level in 1972, but still failed some corporate expectations.

————One gloomy view of profits was provided, in 1972, by the auto companies themselves, in public testimony to the Price Commission. The companies were concerned to demonstrate their need for auto price increases, and GM announced that in 1971 its margin of profit on sales (an economic indicator favored in the auto industry) "was lower than in any year (except the strike year 1970) since the recession of 1958." Ford produced a similar tale of distress: its 1971 profit margin was 4.1 percent of sales, compared to an average of 5.7 percent "for the 30 companies in the Dow-Jones industrial average," and 4.7 percent "for the nation's 500 largest industrial firms"; "unfortunately," the company complained, "our margin is below the average for large corporations."

————Auto employment and profits grew haphazardly in the leaps and falls of the postwar automotive economy. Capital investment moved upwards and downwards: in 1971 GM spent less in real dollars on building new plants and buying new capital equipment than it had spent in 1956, when its real sales were about half as great. Auto productivity, output per hour worked, grew less fast (as measured by the U.S. government) after the Second World War than in the 1920s and 1930s. From 1914 to 1923 the auto industry led the expansion of national productivity; in the 1960s auto productivity grew at exactly the same rate as national industrial productivity, and much less fast than productivity in newer, more expansive industries.

————Even when the auto economy did well, the auto corporations were slow to employ new workers. U.S. auto manufacturers employed more people in 1953 than in any subsequent year. Much of the postwar increase in automotive employment was in the industries that support auto sales: from the Business Census of 1963 to the 1967 Census, total employment in the automotive industries increased by 286,000 jobs—of which only 45,000, or less than one sixth, were in auto and parts manufacturing, while the rest were accounted for at retail and wholesale auto dealerships, gas stations, auto repair shops, parking garages, and auto rental companies. In 1971, President Nixon removed the auto excise tax in an effort, he said, to provide new jobs for Americans. A year later, auto profits and sales were unusually high, but the auto makers' employment had barely increased. GM announced that its worldwide employment had actually fallen during the year; it added that without Nixon's New Economic Policy there would have been more layoffs in the U.S. auto business.

————U.S. auto corporations are losing their international advantages in productivity and sales. Foreign auto industries enjoy the self-generating growth characteristic of the American automotive past. The Japanese auto companies produced 110 cars in 1947, 79,000 cars in 1959, and level of capital investment: at present rates of exchange, 3.2 million cars in 1970. As their home auto markets have increased, foreign corporations have built more and more, newer and newer auto factories. They attract large capital investment, and buy expensive and advanced machinery. From 1967 to 1971, according to *Fortune*'s directories of international corporations, the total dollar assets of the Big Three U.S. auto makers increased by one third, while the total assets of Toyota and Nissan, measured in dollars, increased two and a third times. The international advantages of U.S. corporations have often been based on a high the Japanese auto companies have assets per employee worth more than twice as much as the assets per employee of the three U.S. auto corporations.

————The U.S. companies are themselves expanding their overseas operations much faster than their domestic business. Much of the growth in worldwide employment and investment takes place outside America. GM is less preoccupied than Ford with foreign sales, yet from 1961 to 1971 its U.S. vehicle production increased by a little over three quarters, its German production more than doubled, and its production in Latin America and South Africa increased nearly twelve times.

These automotive trends add up to economic trouble. The U.S. auto business, although enormously powerful and profitable, is now less powerful and less profitable than it has been in the past. The different auto trends seem to follow the same historical pattern: the strategies responsible for the early successes of the auto industry have become, by the 1970s, increasingly inefficient. This pattern is apparent in the many and varied difficulties about which auto executives complain; to see how well it fits the model of the auto business as a depressed American industry it is necessary to look now at the industry's economic development, from the 1920s to its troubled present. The past strength of the auto business was based on Fordism and Sloanism, on the advanced technology of mass production, as applied by the first Henry Ford, and on an early development of elaborate marketing, associated particularly with General Motors. In all the contemporary automotive difficulties, problems of market support and manufacturing technology are perhaps the most ominous. These problems can show to what extent the postwar auto industry has remained faithful to the business strategies of the 1910s, 1920s, and 1930s—and how this loyalty has affected the situation of the auto corporations in the present U.S. economy.

The Ecstatic 1920s

The early history of the auto corporations was described exuberantly by the first auto industrialists. Henry Ford's own memoirs describe the practice and philosophy of the assembly line; Alfred Sloan's business autobiography, *My Years with General Motors*, records the growth of the auto market from its hopeful beginnings to the launching of the Corvair—Sloan, an entrepreneur of roller bearings, was president of General Motors from 1923 to 1941. (More recent developments in the auto economy are harder to discover. As the industry's boom weakened, auto magnates became less outspoken about their business aspirations, and the modern U.S. auto corporations are famously secretive. The companies' annual reports contain general or "consolidated" information; a GM vice-president expressed the industry's attitude to such critical data as rates of growth of productivity when he told the U.S. government Price Commission that he could provide only "a little atmosphere" about GM productivity, since he had been "working with the fellows for fifteen years," trying unsuccessfully to define industrial productivity.)

For the auto industry, the economic boom of the 1920s developed on an ecstatic spiral of demand and supply. Ten thousand Model T's were sold in 1908 and 1909; Ford wrote later that the success of the new car inspired him to buy 60 acres at Highland Park near Detroit, and to make "plans for a bigger factory than the world has ever known." In the middle 1920s, after the ten-millionth Model T was built, Ford was able to boast that "at the Highland Park, we have 25,000 machines. . . ."

The many auto makers of the 1920s had little difficulty in selling all the cars they could produce. By 1930 there was one passenger car registered for every 1.3 American households—in 1910 there had been one car registered for every 44 households. General Motors sold 392,000 vehicles in 1919, and 1,899,000 in 1929; its profits more than tripled in the same period. Because sales and auto production were increasing, the auto corporations' capital investment also increased fast. Each year the companies needed to build new factories, in order to produce more cars. Each factory was more advanced than last year's factory, and employed further refinements of Fordist assembly technology; productivity in the auto industry increased as fast as the flow of newer, bigger, better capital equipment.

Fordism and the New Technology

Ford's auto assembly plants were, in the 1910s and 1920s, the most popular symbols of national industrial progress, of the American machine age. In 1915, enthusiastic crowds at the San Francisco "Palace of Transportation" rioted in their eagerness to see a working replica of Ford's new Highland Park assembly line. Early automotive histories were full of new construction, new factories in new cities. Henry Ford wrote passionately about his mechanized, perpetually reorganized plants, where "hardly a week passes without some improvement being made somewhere in machines or process"; in his best-selling *My Life and Work* he described his own farm childhood in a sentence that became internationally famous, "My toys were all tools —they still are."

From the middle 1910s, sustained by national machine fever, the auto investment boom swerved higher and higher. As Agnelli of Fiat describes it, the U.S. auto business in the 1920s grew faster than national economic production, attracting capital investment from other industrial sectors, and experiencing a "self-generating" momentum in productive and technological expansion. Capital investment in the auto industry grew many times faster than capital in other American industries, where demand was increasing less euphorically. From 1914 to 1919 the value of invested capital in the motor vehicle industry increased more than 300 percent, while the value of all manufacturing capital increased by about 25 percent. From 1914 to 1929, automotive capital increased in value almost 3 times as fast as all manufacturing capital, 4½ times as fast as capital in the machinery industry, and more than 6 times as fast as capital in the older iron and steel industry.

"Fordism," the technology of mass assembly-line production, was made possible by this rapid expansion of output and capital investment. The new technology was based on machinery, and on the "rational" reorganization of work to fit the rhythm of the new machinery. Ford wrote that "the work and the work alone controls us"; in accordance with the theories of Frederick Winslow Taylor, all possible skills were transferred from human workers to machines, from people to automatic tools and to the moving assembly line. Many parts of Ford's automobiles were put together mechanically, and those jobs which still required some human "knack" or adaptability were reduced to their smallest, fastest, least wasteful components, "dividing and subdividing operations, keeping the work in motion—these are the keynotes of production." In the new organization of auto production, unskilled workers were seen by management as rather simple machines which happened to be alive—Henry Ford expressed this attitude most clearly in his description of factory life: "A business is men and machines united in the production of a commodity and both the men and the machines need repairs and replacements. . . . Machinery wears out and needs to be restored. Men grow uppish, lazy, or careless. . . ."

After the 1920s investment boom, the auto corporation began to find increasing difficulty in improving the efficiency of Fordist technology—and they also, of course, found considerable difficulties in "labor relations" with their employees. Fordist production seemed to be approaching an almost physical limitation. Machines had taken over more and more jobs in auto and parts manufacturing, and by the 1930s there were comparatively few new functions to be mechanized. Cars were still made of thousands of metal parts, welded or bolted together: even in the automation boom of the 1950s much of the auto corporations' investment, particularly in assembly factories, consisted of improving *control* over operations that had already been mechanized, often as long as thirty years before. Meanwhile, as the auto industry faced these investment limitations, other, newer industries had developed technologies that allowed a much greater increase in capital and productivity, with, often, much greater variety and responsibility in production work. The process industries, for example (such as the chemical, petroleum, and electricity businesses, where goods flow continuously and more or less automatically through a factory, their production regulated by electronic controls rather than by unskilled work), by the 1950s and 1960s were acquiring new capital much faster than the auto business, and used many times more capital equipment for every worker. For the auto corporations, because of technical necessity and also, perhaps, because of management attitudes to production work, modern Fordism had come to mean less and less Fordist mechanization—with more and more Fordist reorganization of work.

After the Depression

The early auto boom ended with the Great Depression. Cars were the first luxuries that people stopped buying after 1929, and the car population fell as millions of Americans sold or junked the cars they could no longer afford to keep. The credit structure which had supported the auto sales boom of the 1920s collapsed: in 1930 between one third and one fourth of all U.S. auto dealers went out of business. Of the 475,000 auto workers in Detroit in 1929, 125,000 were laid off in 1930 and another 100,000 in 1931. Two thirds of the working population, and an almost unbelievable 80 per cent of all blacks, was wholly or partly unemployed in Detroit. Ford Motor Company complained that its few remaining auto workers were weak from hunger, and vulnerable to infection; by 1932 nearly one in five of all Detroit schoolchildren was officially recognized as seriously undernourished.

In the middle 1930s the profits of the auto corporations began to recover—although unemployment in Detroit remained high until 1942, when the auto factories started war production (of tanks, guns, aircraft, ammunition), and auto sales did not again reach their 1929 level until 1949. The 1935–37 recovery had little of the optimism of the industry's glorious past. It was characterized by determined cost-cutting, by struggle between management and workers, and by a new corporate emphasis on techniques for stimulating consumer demand.

Ford in the early 1920s made about half of all cars sold in America, and General Motors about one quarter; by the middle 1930s the position was reversed. The transition from Ford leadership to GM leadership can stand for the general transformation of the industry. Henry Ford wrote passionately about the 1920s, about industrial and engineering expansion, about the falling prices of his Model T's. (Ford prices were cut six times between 1921 and 1925, and in 1924 the most popular Ford touring car cost $290— or the equivalent of $700 in today's money.) Alfred Sloan of GM wrote with similar rapture about his company's expansion in the 1930s, about the development and elaboration of the car market, about the rising quality and rising prices of GM cars, their bright colors and sculptured lines. Sloan has described the early auto situation as balanced between the philosophy of Henry Ford and the philosophy of William C. Durant, GM's founder and apostle, and Sloan's own mentor: "Mr. Ford's assembly-line automobile production, high minimum wage, and low-priced car were revolutionary and stand among the greatest contributions to our industrial culture. His basic conception of one car in one utility model at an ever lower price was what the market, especially the farm market, mainly needed at the time. Yet Mr. Durant's feeling for variety in automobiles . . . came closer to the trend of the industry as it evolved in later years." By 1935 the GM principles of variety marketing were dominant in the U.S. auto business.

Sloanism, or GM's Variety Marketing

GM spent comparatively little on new capital equipment in the 1930s; Sloan boasted that the company was able to meet the expansion of auto demand in 1935–37 with mod-

est investment, and by "reactivating" old factories that had
been closed down in 1930. Total vehicle sales during the
recovery were well below the 1929 peak—GM used its
corporate energies on new sales techniques to inflect this
mediocre market, achieving a growing share of all auto
sales, and making sure that it derived a satisfactory profit
from the cars it sold. Alfred Sloan was himself the major
prophet of GM's new sales policy. He laid down the company's marketing principles, as formulated in the 1920s
and applied after the Depression: "The primary object of
the corporation," he proclaimed, "was to make money, not
just to make motor cars": "The core of the [GM] product
policy [lay] in its concept of mass-producing a full line of
cars graded upward in quality and price. . . . In later years,
as the consumer upgraded his preference, the new General
Motors policy was to become critically attuned to the course
of American history."

Sloan's idea for upgrading consumer preferences was
that automobiles should change each year, and should each
year become more expensive (at least relative to the cost
of production). The rate at which people traded in their
old cars would grow. Each year, the new-model cars would
have more improvements added on, different engines, different styling, different comfort features. Cars of the same
shape and size, made from the same basic metal parts,
could be sold with different equipment, at different prices.
In the early 1930s, GM reduced its production to "three
basic standard types" of auto bodies, but aspired to offer
"the greatest possible diversity" of auto models: Alfred
Sloan wrote that "It is perfectly possible, from the engineer-

ing and manufacturing standpoint, to make two cars at not a great difference in price and weight, but considerably different in appearance. . . ." On this strategy, the auto companies could continue to make large profits even when demand (and production, and investment, and productivity) was growing only slowly. GM's new policy was soon successful: in 1935 the company made more profit after tax (in real dollars, adjusted for changes in the value of money) for every vehicle it produced than it had made in the record year 1929. (This figure measures the ratio of total profits to total vehicle production, not the profit made *on* the sale of each vehicle.)

The expansion of consumer credit in the 1920s and 1930s was led by the auto industry, and by the General Motors Acceptance Corporation, which financed the purchase of automobiles by dealers and customers. Alfred Sloan described the need for installment selling: banks did not "take kindly to" the "broad approach" to consumer financing, so "some other means had to be found if the auto industry was to sell cars in large numbers." The cyclical trading of used cars as down payments on new cars had, as Sloan put it, "revolutionary significance not only for dealer arrangements but for manufacturing and the whole character of production."

Many of the characteristic "improvements" of the modern automobile were first applied in the 1930s. The Sculptured Design. The Brightly Colored Body. The Large Engine. The Low, Lean Look. The Annual Model Change: Sloan writes that ". . . the fact that we made yearly changes, and the recognition of the necessity of change, forced us into regularizing change. When change became regularized, sometime in the 1930s, we began to speak of annual models." GM's famous "Art and Color" Section, later the Styling Division, was established in 1927 but first flourished in the 1930s. Sloan describes the "stimulating atmosphere in the early 1930s" at the Art and Color room of the GM building in Detroit, where "executives mingled with designers, engineers, woodworkers, clay modelers," looking at car designs on blackboards "which, surrounded by black velvet curtains, made the white body lines stand out sharply." (These were the years, it will be recalled, when two thirds of the working population of Detroit was unemployed.)

On the basis of GM's strategy for "upgrading" the American automobile, U.S. auto marketing became a worldwide model for the selling of expensive consumer goods, showing businesses how to create and nourish demand. Refrigerators, stoves, television sets, electric typewriters are now, each year, better, fancier, and more expensive. The GM strategy also had much the same relationship to subsequent automotive history as Fordist assembly-line technology had to the development of auto engineering. Sloanist principles of perpetual improvement and elaboration dominated the auto market of the 1950s and 1960s. The wild transformations of annual styling changes, the chrome insignia and giant engines of the 1950s, the stereo tape-players, power equipment, and air conditioners of the 1960s were foreseen in Sloan's early policy. Yet GM after the Depression was selling to consumers who had often known only the functional and uncomfortable 1920s Ford cars. Variety salesmanship, as will be seen, proved more and more troublesome in the increasingly jaded postwar auto market.

Postwar Vicissitudes

The auto industry led the expansion of consumer demand at the end of the Second World War. (Auto factories were turned over to war production after 1942, but GM, at least, planned its postwar growth throughout the war years. A momentous wartime episode, as described by Alfred Sloan, concerned the automotive Tailfin—which was conceived when GM's chief stylist went to visit a friend in the airforce, saw some new fighter planes equipped with twin tailfins, and in an instant of creativity intuited the future history of auto rear ends.) Car sales passed their 1929 level in 1949; in 1950 the auto corporations made more cars than they made in 1970, and established a new record which was reached only once again in the 1950s.

The 1950 boom was followed at once by the first of the many recessions which have shaped the automotive economy ever since. In the ten years after 1951 the industry suffered five small slumps, followed by a boom and two serious depressions between 1961 and 1971. During these slumps, all the economic indicators of automotive growth fluctuated together. GM's sales, profits, employment, and capital investment boomed and fell. To take a few examples, GM's capital investment (in real money) was higher in 1956 than in 1971; its profits hardly grew between 1955 and 1962; its U.S. vehicle production was lower in 1970 than in 1965, 1960, 1955, or 1950; its U.S. employment was about the same in 1970 as in 1955.

The auto corporations could never rely upon the more or less uninterrupted market growth that they had enjoyed before 1930. Auto sales, profits, investment were disrupted

again and again by crises of national demand. Whenever
the auto companies attempted major investment programs
they were overtaken by yet another slump in consumer
morale; in 1956, for example, GM completed its most important postwar capital expansion project—by the next
recession, in 1958, GM's new investment had fallen back
to one third of its 1956 level. The gloomy result of these
postwar fluctuations was that the automotive economy developed increasingly disappointingly—on a depressive spiral, where the forces of the 1920s boom moved in reverse.
Demand, and auto production, grew slowly and haphazardly; profits were often unsatisfactory; the auto business
attracted less and less investment from other economic sectors; capital expenditure grew slowly because the future
expansion of output was uncertain; the rate of technological
growth was only as fast as the slow flow of new capital
equipment; productivity increased slowly.

A major reason for the postwar fluctuations of the automotive economy was the unreliability of consumer demand
for automobiles. By the early 1950s the U.S. auto market
was moving towards saturation in the ratio of people to
automobiles. There were more passenger cars in America
than there were households—one car for every 3¾ Americans, or a greater auto density than is to be found almost
anywhere else in the world today. Over the next twenty
years, sometimes fast and sometimes slowly, the auto corporations were able to push auto saturation to its present
level of one car for every 2¼ people. Yet the fact that the
companies were operating always so near the limits of
(plausible) market saturation made them especially vulnerable to changes in the national economy. Auto sales

suffered early in each postwar recession: consumers were always quick to forgo car radios or extra chrome, to put off buying their second or third family car, to postpone trading in last year's cars for newer, improved models.

Sloanism Continued

Through the vicissitudes of the postwar economy, the auto industry has continued to rely on GM's early strategies for automotive upgrading. The variety marketing of the 1950s and 1960s would have surpassed William Durant's wildest hopes. The "value," elaboration, and price of American automobiles rose continually—in the planned obsolescence of the 1950s, the fashions for huge cars, muscular cars, sporty cars, the 1960s explosion of optional, extra-cost auto accessories. The auto market became a market for automobiles, auto spare parts, cigarette lighters, radios, stereos, carpets, chrome ornaments, vinyl roof coverings, power equipment, air conditioners, safety belts, exhaust catalysts ... a market whose cash value was increasing notably faster than the number of cars sold.

The auto companies, by their development of the upgrading strategy, made sure that their total annual sales fluctuated much less than annual auto production, or than total annual profits. The average wholesale cost of an American auto increased from $1,300 in 1949 to $1,880 in 1959, $2,280 in 1969, and $2,500 in 1971; between 1919 and 1929 it had fallen by $200, from $830 to $630. Alfred Sloan's autobiography ends with a chapter called "Change and Progress," in which Sloan quotes with approval a pas-

sage from *Fortune* magazine of 1953: "In the postwar
sellers' market, [the auto industry] has found itself selling
more car per car—more accessories, luxuries, improvements, and innovations. Now it has to plan it that way. . . .
The widening spread between unit demand and purchasing
power will create a powerful drive to sell still more car per
unit." By producing varieties of auto parts, as well as automobiles, the auto companies were able to protect themselves
from some of the terrors of national economic fluctuations:
when times were bad, people would put off buying new cars,
but would buy spare parts to keep their old cars on the roads,
and when times were good, people would buy cars loaded
with optional extras. (The attractions of the auto-parts
market were known to the early auto industry: in 1932,
the worst year of the Depression, GM had a $7 million loss
on motor vehicle sales, but a $10 million profit on acces-
sories and parts.)

Modern upgrading, and "selling more car per car," made
it possible for the auto companies to maintain the value of
the auto market; in order to increase auto sales they developed, by contrast, a new style of variety marketing, the
marketing of second and third cars. From 1950 to 1970,
the companies managed to increase the passenger-car population of America less than half as fast as it increased in
the 1920s—but nearly three times faster than the increase
in the human population. The proportion of American families owning more than one car grew from 7 percent in
1950 to 15 percent in 1960 and 29 percent in 1970. In the
1960s, the total number of car-owning families barely
changed, while the car population increased substantially—
almost the entire extra demand for cars came from families

that decided to buy second or third cars. Some contemporary cars, including, as will be seen, the Chevrolet Vega,
are designed and sold as blatant second cars, for women,
teenagers, and special occasions. The U.S. auto industry now anticipates a perpetual trading up in car ownership. If auto executives have to talk
about saturation, they talk about the ratio of cars to drivers,
not about the ratio of cars to people, or to families.* In their
optimistic scenario, husbands need cars for driving to work,
and wives for going shopping, and teenage children for trips
to school or to the local entertainment mall. The family
might need a larger car (or a recreational vehicle) for vacation trips; some lucky drivers can use two or more cars, and
can rent yet other vehicles. According to the *Wall Street
Journal*, "Detroit marketing men figure a one-to-one ratio
[of cars to drivers] may be the limit, but even that may be
elastic because 'it assumes that each driver doesn't own or
use more than one car,' as one official puts it." This vision
could be more than the fantasy of an effervescent automotive
imagination: a report on environmental problems commis-
sioned by the White House suggests that, because of the
expense of federal antipollution regulations, American
drivers might adopt a "2-car strategy," buying one low-
pollution urban vehicle, and one nonurban car; the report
was acclaimed by the delighted president of Ford Motor
Company as possibly "the best news the public has had in
years."

---

* They could thus argue that while, say, Burma may be one five-hun-
dredth as saturated automotively as the United States, with one passenger car for every thousand people, it probably also suffers from a
national shortage of qualified drivers.

Variety marketing, in its two manifestations of automotive upgrading and multicar salesmanship, worked fairly well for the auto corporations during the economic fluctuations between the middle 1930s and the middle 1960s. But in the last few years, as America becomes ever more saturated with autos, and as American autos become ever more saturated with auto accessories, even variety marketing has turned increasingly troublesome. For people outside the auto industry (or the White House) an orderly national trade-up towards multicar ownership seems unlikely. *Fortune* complains that it can no longer predict systematically the future growth of the auto market; in the 1970s, it says, the forces affecting automotive demand will be mysterious, or political, social, medical (ecological), and technological; American families may no longer as a matter of course buy extra cars when their children learn to drive, or when the head of the household gets a raise, and they may even move away from the suburbs, and forget to replace their old family sedan.

The auto-accessories market presents similar problems. Many of the auto improvements of the 1950s and 1960s are themselves approaching saturation. Automatic transmissions and car radios are installed on 80 to 90 percent of all new cars. American cars are fast, comfortable, and temperate. The tailfin has been discredited, and cars are too powerful even for the acceleration lanes of urban freeways. 1973 Cadillacs offer "new niceties you may add. Like a lighted vanity mirror for the lady. An outside thermometer. A laprobe and pillow...." The auto companies expect to sell new accessories in the 1970s, including possible "safety" options, but these add-ons are not likely to re-create the marketing euphoria of the chrome-loaded 1950s. In the 1970s, then, the U.S. auto corporations can expect to face more and more serious problems in their automotive marketing. On the Sloanist policy for relentless automotive upgrading, the auto corporations must persuade consumers to spend at least a constant proportion of their "widening" incomes ("purchasing power") on autos and auto appurtenances. This proportion has remained fairly steady since the Second World War, at least until the last few years. Yet in 1972, a boom year for the industry, GM itself complained that "the steady stream of other new products and services competing for the consumer dollar in recent years is providing new dimensions of competition [for auto sales]." As national income grows, constant proportional auto spending requires growing total auto spending, and more cars per driver, with more options per car. As of 1972, it seems uncertain that Americans will continue to spend a constant tenth of their growing incomes on buying more and more cars to drive on the foul and congested roads—and on supporting, upgrading, and bedecking their automobiles. There is perpetually, for the auto companies of the 1970s, a danger that next year or next decade the limits of the car market may collide with the limits of human irrationality.

Fordism Continued

The postwar auto corporations found as many problems with auto production and productivity as they found in their automotive marketing. The depressive spiral of haphazard growth, led by the slow increase of auto demand in a congested market, had gloomy repercussions for auto engineering. All the forces of early automotive expansion worked in reverse. Where auto technology once stood for national industrial progress, auto production now seems unexciting, and no crowds fight to see Ford's new assembly lines. Where the early auto industry led the national economy in growth of capital investment and productivity, the contemporary industry advances much less fast than many younger businesses, and often less fast than the average for all national business.

According to the U.S. government's historical statistics, output per manhour (or productivity) in the motor vehicle industry grew about 8.6 percent a year between 1919 and 1930: notably faster than the growth of productivity in the whole private economy, or than in any other major American industry—productivity for the whole economy grew 1.9 percent a year, for the steel industry 5.8 percent a year, and for the steam railroad industry 1.7 percent a year. Postwar measurements of productivity are only approximately comparable (and, probably, only approximately accurate), but the relative positions of different industries are clearly transformed: between 1960 and 1971 productivity in the motor vehicle industry increased 3 percent a year, in all private industry also 3 percent a year, in the radio and television receiver industry 6.9 percent a year, and in the oil pipeline business about 10 percent a year.

The same pattern is shown in the growth of auto investment. The modern auto companies invest less than they used to, and less than corporations in other industries. From 1918 to 1920 GM invested $280 million in new plant and equipment, or 20 percent of its total sales value; the company now spends about 4 percent of the value of its sales on capital equipment. Meanwhile, other American industries experience the spiraling expansion which the auto companies enjoyed in the 1920s. For the modern computer, advanced-electronics, or petroleum industries, demand, technology, investment, and productivity have grown together. Throughout the 1960s, the motor-vehicle and parts group had one of the lowest rates of growth of assets per employee of any manufacturing industry group listed in the *Fortune* 500 directory: from 1961 to 1971 GM's assets per employee increased 47 percent, Exxon's 86 percent, and Dow Chemical's also 86 percent.

When the modern auto companies announce expansionary investment programs, they emphasize styling changes rather than advances in productive technology or productive capacity. According to the industry, for example, the major 1950s expansion of auto capital was required because of changes in consumer preferences, the new fashion for faster engines and larger, more comfortable, and more elaborate cars. Henry Ford and his contemporaries saw capital expansion as a thrilling and profitable adventure; for modern auto industrialists it is a regrettable necessity. This new attitude is expressed clearly by Lee A. Iacocca, the present president of Ford Motor Company. Iacocca, who believes that Japan is "where the action is" in the modern auto business, has argued that American problems of national productivity arise from the reluctance of American businessmen, as compared to Japanese businessmen, to invest new capital. Yet when Iacocca describes his own company's investment plans, he sounds surprisingly jaded. He recently told the Los Angeles Chamber of Commerce that improving productivity "requires a good bit of cash. As I'm sure you all know, productivity in manufacturing involves more automation, more systematic integration of operations, reduced idle time, and so forth. . . ."

The auto industry has reacted to its new problem of productivity in much the same way as it reacted to the saturation of auto demand: by turning in upon itself, towards a more intensive application of the policies responsible for its early successes. Modern auto marketing is Sloanist upgrading upgraded—modern auto technology relies on a similar development of Fordist processes. All the productive improvements mentioned by Iacocca, "reduced idle time, and so forth," are derived from Fordist theory; another contemporary Ford executive, asked about the possibility of restructuring assembly-line technology, has said that the Ford company does not think it necessary "to retreat from the pioneering work of [the first] Henry Ford."

In the 1970s, as in the 1920s and 1930s, the auto companies are determined to cut production costs, a penny here and a penny there. They search for idle moments to be filled, and for idle movements to be reorganized. The search becomes harder, but the companies are ever more determined: a determination which is shown in the Lordstown production of GM's Vega. For all American business, the auto industry has become a model of managerial intransigence. An article in *Business Week*, called "Aerospace Copies Detroit," describes how two former auto executives transformed the diversified aircraft corporation, North American Rockwell. The two auto managers instituted "rigid one-year plans" for evaluating profit performance, visited research and development groups "at least once a week [to] ask what their costs were," fired about half of the corporation's central staff, including "pool secretaries and chauffeurs," and complained that previous management had been "all wrapped up in its technical underwear"; Detroit, *Business Week* commented, is "celebrated for [its] preoccupation with cost-cutting through tight managerial control."

In 1929, Alfred Sloan urged General Motors "to put the energy previously directed towards expansion and development into the hardest kind of drive in the direction of economy"—and it is still the case that immense automotive energy is spent on economy, perhaps at the expense of changes in technology and work. The auto philosophy of permanent, intensive reorganization is summed up in the business personalities of present auto magnates. Richard Gerstenberg, the chairman of GM, is thought to have achieved his present position because of his reputation as a dedicated cutter of costs. His first job at GM, in 1932, was as a timekeeper, with special responsibility for collecting time clocks. He apparently adhered to principles of hard economy during his long progress through the financial and budgetary departments of GM, and his corporate elevation was welcomed in the auto industry with such observations as that "the situation calls for a cost-cutter, rather than a product developer and innovator." Gerstenberg described his own business beliefs in an interview given to *Automotive News* just before he became GM's chairman: "We think we've been pretty damn good at cost control over the years. If there's one thing we work at every day, it's the control of costs. But you can always find ways to improve."

The recent history of the automotive economy suggests that the American auto companies face at least a relative decline in their economic vigor and profitability; that the auto business is a maturing industry, operating in the same way that it did in its youth, but with less success—fixed obsessively on an early pattern of production and sales.

The auto industry now appears as a troubled sector of American business. It depends upon the Fordist technology of mass production—and its rate of growth of productivity falls behind that of many newer industries. It sells upgraded cars—and the automotive share of national consumer spending seems ever more uncertain, as more and more people buy services, or newer consumer products. These problems continue beyond the cyclical fluctuations of the auto economy: the industry's technological inertia has become more pronounced in the last ten or twenty years; in the 1972 auto boom, while GM executives complained about competition for the consumer dollar, consumers spent just over 7 percent of their income on automobiles, auto parts, and mobile homes, about the same percentage as in previous booms of 1965 and 1955—but spending on services, such as medical care, recreation, and personal care, had increased significantly since those earlier booms.

Past auto development can help to explain the more mysterious of modern automotive problems. Consumer discontent with automotive culture and with the complexities of auto selling has an evident relation to Sloanist strategy, where the industry attempts, in increasing frenzy, to persuade people to buy more cars than they want, with more accessories than they need. The unreliability and dangers of automobiles, and the congestion of cities and suburbs may seem particularly unsatisfactory, where so much of American life—going to work or to school or to market—requires auto transportation. Consumer attitudes may reflect corporate behavior, and the auto-based organization of the national economy; to see this is not to downgrade the national movement against congestion, pollution, and automotive hyperbole, but simply to understand the movement's strength.

The same sort of observations will seem relevant to accounts of auto workers' discontent. Auto workers revolt not only because they are young, or (comparatively) "affluent"—but also because the American auto industry's production policy consists of an increasingly arduous organization of factory work, an increasingly determined reduction of factory costs. Jobs in modern auto factories are still based on Fordist regimentation, and the modern auto companies are still increasing the regimentation of work. To see how plausibly these arguments can explain present auto troubles, it is now appropriate to look at practical examples of automotive policy: at the selling of the Chevrolet Vega, as an example of variety marketing in conditions of advanced market congestion; and at the Lordstown Vega factories, as an example of modern times in auto technology.

3
American Selling: The Vega

The selling of GM's Chevrolet Vega is a pure example of modern Sloanism. Described by GM as the "direct result of the most expensive program of scientific market analysis ever undertaken by General Motors," the Vega displays the achievements and contradictions of the saturated American auto market. The short history of the Vega is already famous: the new, small car was launched in 1970 as an all-American defense against the frighteningly successful German and Japanese cars; it was manufactured at the unprecedentedly expensive and "advanced" Lordstown factories; it was chosen in 1972 as the first American car to be powered (probably in 1974) by a Wankel engine; in its first two years it suffered three major recalls for safety defects, developed many smaller deficiencies, and was criticized by the American consumer movement with an urgency unknown since the downfall of the Chevrolet Corvair.

Through all its tribulations, the Vega was supported by

GM's newest techniques of advertising and market expansion. The techniques were even adjusted for consumer discontent, and Vega marketing was based on an expensive and intensive soft sell (a sell which stressed economy and reliability, to the subsequent embarrassment of Chevrolet). The Vega market can show how Sloanist selling works under modern adversity—its relation to foreign competition, its economic and advertising appeal, and its "problems" with auto safety. It can also indicate some of the more general contradictions of automotive selling, where cars are necessities of life, but also overpriced and overelaborate, in the most overdeveloped of all consumer markets.

In the winter of 1970 imported cars had captured a larger part of the U.S. market than ever before. Until the advent of the Vega and its coeval Ford Pinto (and American Motors Gremlin), the U.S. auto manufacturers produced no domestic small cars to compete with foreign subcompacts: Volkswagen sales had doubled from 1968 to 1970, while Toyota sales tripled; in late 1970 Japanese automobiles seemed alarmingly strong in Los Angeles. The struggle between U.S. and foreign small cars seemed a symbol of economic peril—as one GM executive put it, a "relevant example of what is happening to American industry in the world marketplace."

Chevrolet aimed its Vega directly at this fearful national mood. The car had been described first, in 1968, by the chairman of GM, as "GM's positive answer to the demonstrated need for a small, economical, durable, safe, comfortable, and well-styled car built in America to American tastes." In September 1970 the Vega went on sale with even more impressive patriotic credentials: according to J. Z. DeLorean, then head of Chevrolet, GM had "set out to produce an American car [the Vega] with size, economy, and performance to serve the American people. . . . We set out to improve this country's balance of payments."

The new car was designed, quite openly, to appeal to people who might otherwise have bought foreign cars. GM financed an elaborate "national probability study," to discover why Americans liked imported cars. The size and appearance of the Vega was determined largely by these investigations—as DeLorean put it, "we held product clinics with small-car enthusiasts as we finalized our designs." The Vega looks like a Fiat: one motoring magazine commented that GM should be paying a styling fee to Pininfarina. Even its name was exotic. Vega: sounds Italian. 2300: for engine capacity in cubic centimeters, a foreign measure, as in BMW 2500, or Alfa Romeo 1750 Berlina. (In the 1973 model year, Chevrolet dropped the number 2300—apparently because customers thought it referred to the dollar price of the new, cheap car.) Meanwhile, company publicists referred coyly to the Volkswagen as Brand X, claiming that the Vega would have "nearly twice the power of the leading foreign import."

The launching of the Vega stimulated much anxious debate about the appeal of foreign cars. Were American multicar families becoming bored with home-made automobiles? Did they buy imports simply for their foreignness; could the jaded tastes of the second-car consumer be titillated only by outlandish commodities? *Automotive News* remembered the lost days of the mid-fifties, when imported cars "were oddities to buy capriciously and own defensively." GM's probability study had revealed, encouragingly enough, that "over 60 percent of those owning foreign economy cars said they would be willing to consider buying domestic small cars." But auto executives worried about other, mysterious advantages of foreign cars. Did consumers have an "image," as they paid for their Toyotas, of diligent Japanese auto workers singing company songs and building high-quality cars? DeLorean provided many such explanations for what he called the "mystique" of the Volkswagen: "The foreign-car buyer," he complained, "has an image of craftsmen in the Black Forest, building cars by hand."

In the first year of the Vega, these corporate speculations developed into a major campaign of automotive xenophobia (as Toyota sales increased 74 percent, from August 1970 to August 1971, when foreign cars captured more than 20 percent of the U.S. market). The U.S. auto makers adopted an aggressive strategy of attacking foreign cars—a strategy which, as will be shown later, recalls most vividly the chauvinism of depressed British manufacturers in 1900, warning against cheap German textiles and machinery. Mr. DeLorean said cryptically, in the spring of 1971, that "the only way to handle the Japanese" was "to have our own [Chevrolet's] fleet of submarines." At the 1971 Ford shareholders meeting, Henry Ford II conceded that the Pinto and the Vega had so far failed to "stem the tide" of imported cars. Things would get worse, and the United States might become a "service-oriented" country. The Japanese, Ford said, had so far concentrated their auto-selling efforts on the East and West coasts: "Wait till [the Japanese] get a hold of the central part of the United States, then see what they will do." (These are Ford's words as quoted in the *Washington Post*. The *Wall Street Journal* reported his remarks as follows: "Just wait until the Jobs [*sic*] get into mid-America with broad distribution of their cars.")

Ford Motor Company supported its chairman's geopolitical warnings with an advertising campaign urging consumers to buy "domestic small cars [such as Ford Pintos] designed and engineered from the outset to be driven by American-size people on American-type roads." Why were foreign cars unsatisfactory? Because, the advertisements proclaimed, the "average American is 4.3 inches taller and 31 pounds heavier than the average Japanese." The auto industry invoked the direst visions of Toyotas in Pearl Harbor, Santa Monica, the American heartland. . . . *Car and Driver* magazine summed up this automotive chauvinism when it published a full-page photograph of an American beach (Waikiki? Malibu?) with a solitary Japanese businessman standing on the sand. He holds a briefcase and a calling card, and smiles slightly; he has apparently waded ashore in his neat, dark suit. On the next page, there are five identical Japanese salesmen standing on the beach with their business cards; they almost obscure the vista of the Pacific Ocean.

The immediate and most famous result of the auto campaign against foreign cars came in August 1971, in the shape of President Nixon's New Economic Policy. The August economic package was presented as a special handout for the U.S. auto business, and two days after the New Policy was announced, GM, Ford, Chrysler, and American

Motors were the four most upwardly active shares on the New York Stock Exchange. President Nixon explained one part of the package, the effective devaluation of the dollar, in terms of its encouraging effect on the domestic auto industry. He wanted to "lay to rest the bugaboo of devaluation." "What does this action mean for you? If you want to buy a foreign car, or take a trip abroad, market conditions may cause your dollar to buy slightly less. But if you are among the overwhelming majority who buy American-made products in America your dollar will be worth just as much tomorrow as it is today."

Nixon's policy for domestic expansion was similarly partial. Removal of the 7 percent federal excise tax on automobiles accounted for more than a third of the entire domestic program: even *Automotive News* commented that Treasury Secretary John B. Connally "sounded almost like an industry public relations man when he noted the inequity of the tax," and it pointed out that "the telephone excise tax is also inequitable and almost as large." Not surprisingly, repeal of the 7 percent excise tax had been suggested often by the auto industry's highest officers. Three days before Nixon's August speech, the chairman of Chrysler had addressed reporters in Land of the Ozarks, Missouri, about the prospects for the national economy. Repeal of the auto excise tax, he said, would be "one thing that could really kick off the national economic upturn."

The New Economic Policy was successful, at least temporarily, in improving automotive fortunes. GM executives claimed in July 1972 that the "inroads of foreign manufacturers" had been "checked": they thanked the President for the "worldwide currency realignments [which had] substantially improved the competitive price position of domestically produced smaller passenger cars"—making basic Vegas and Pintos, at last, cheaper than basic Volkswagens, Toyotas and Datsuns. Foreign cars still accounted for almost 15 percent of the 1972 auto market, as compared to 15.1 percent in 1971, 14.7 percent in 1970, and under 10 percent from 1965 to 1969; but with auto profits inflated in the national economic boom, and with Pintos and Vegas selling adequately well, the auto manufacturers were ready at last to relax their patriotic vigilance.

In corporate rhetoric, the changing menace of foreign cars was the subject of an orderly history, beginning in 1969 in the Black Forest, and ending with the Nixon boom of 1972. Yet much of this rhetoric now seems disingenuous, and even the auto manufacturers' panic bore little relation to economic reality. International auto troubles were at once minimized and exaggerated: foreign competition existed before 1969, and continues after 1972, while the problems of the U.S. auto market go beyond international readjustment. The large U.S. manufacturers have been a major force in the world auto market at least since Henry Ford in 1919 built an auto factory in his family's home town of Cork, Southern Ireland, or since General Motors bought Opel in 1929, or since the Tokyo earthquake of 1923, when Ford sold 1,000 American buses to the distressed municipality. The foreign subsidiaries of U.S. companies participated eagerly in the international menace of 1970 and 1971; while Ford advertisements in 1971 were describing the diminutive physique of Japanese motorists, Ford executives were searching longingly for a Japanese alliance, GM executives were actually arranging such an alliance, and Chrysler was importing into the United States thousands of small Japanese cars.

Recent auto troubles, as shown in the Vega project, have more to do with market congestion and technological inertia than with foreign inscrutability. Foreign cars have been important in the U.S. auto market since the late 1950s. In 1960, as in 1970, domestic auto makers were forced to produce a range of comparatively small cars, to compete with cheap imports. These cars, the original compacts such as Chevrolet's Corvair and Ford's Falcon, were successful in reducing the market share of Volkswagen and other European manufacturers. Then, during the economic boom of the middle 1960s, and in accordance with Sloanist principles of perpetual upgrading, the American compacts became larger, more elaborate, and more expensive. By the depressed late 1960s, consumers were again ready to buy small, cheap cars, imported from Europe or Japan. The new appeal of Volkswagens and Toyotas was not entirely mysterious: until the domestic "subcompacts" went on sale, the only available automobiles that were less than 180 inches long and cost less than $2,300 were foreign-made. (Some of these cars were the "captive" imports made abroad by the foreign subsidiaries and associates of American manufacturers. In the year of most extravagant national peril, from August 1970 to August 1971, such cars flourished: GM's German-made "Buick" Opel was the fourth most popular imported car; sales of captive imports increased 78 percent over the year, while sales of other, independent foreign cars increased 48 percent, and sales of U.S.-made cars increased 8 percent. Various auto components were also made abroad: early Vegas featured German manual transmissions, while some early Pintos had engines from the German Ford Capri, carburetors from the English Ford Cortina, Anglo-German transmissions, and steering gear from the European Ford Escort.)

The relative cheapness of foreign cars was, as much as their appeal, a consequence of domestic economic problems. A major reason for the competitiveness of foreign cars was the efficiency of foreign manufacturers, who had experienced in the 1950s and 1960s the rapid growth of markets and productivity enjoyed by the U.S. industry thirty years before. Foreign companies bought the new and expensive capital equipment that domestic corporations felt unable to afford: the superior productivity of some foreign producers was recognized by those U.S. executives who felt that Japan was where the action was, and by the general manager of the General Motors Assembly Division, who in 1972 told a newspaper reporter that "In my judgment, our division doesn't compare with the Japanese in productivity."

Some managers blamed price differentials on high U.S. wage rates, on the fact that foreign manufacturers enjoy "labor costs one half to one quarter as much as ours." But a senior Ford executive explained in August 1970 that "hourly wages don't make the difference any more between manufacturers in different countries. The difference lies in techniques and production volume." According to this executive, "If you add up all the elements of a car, from tires to engine, glass, seats, etc. (without counting raw material), the total number of working hours embodied in a car is between 65 and 70." On these figures, the wage cost in 1970 of the labor needed to produce a Vega would be around $300. The wage cost of making a Volkswagen might have been $150, and of a Toyota $75 (if German and Japanese wage rates were respectively one half and one quarter as high as U.S. rates). Yet in 1970, according to the *Wall Street Journal*, the average cost of importing a car into America, in transportation expenses and customs duty, was $150: a cost which would cancel the labor-cost advantage of Volkswagens and leave a $75 cost advantage for Toyotas. The labor-cost differential between U.S. and foreign manufacturers was in any case rather less than that estimated by U.S. managers, and is less now than it was in 1970. Productive efficiency remains a more important cause of international auto-cost differences.

The apparently mysterious consumer preference for foreign cars (Ford's "pro-foreign, anti-Detroit syndrome") seemed based on rational choice—a consequence of U.S. productive failings, and of market elaboration. Foreign companies could sometimes provide auto varieties not otherwise available, as with their cheap cars in 1959 and 1969, and as they are likely to do in future auto depressions. Yet like the Vega and the Pinto, imported Volkswagens and Toyotas were intended to stimulate the tastes of the young, or of women, or of second-car consumers; like Vegas and Pintos, they were also progressively upgraded in the 1972 auto boom. Auto importers shared the domestic manufacturers' basic problem, of selling ever more cars per family, with ever more accessories per car. Except in the rhetoric of corporate chauvinism, foreign competition was an expected manifestation of general auto troubles: Vegas, beyond their patriotic virtues, were all-purpose modern cars,

and their history before, during, and after the recent crisis
of foreign competition can show most clearly the development of Sloanist marketing in America.

The Vega was famous for years before its public appearance in September 1970. It had been the subject of the
longest prenatal advertising campaign ever provided by
American business. Even its name was a matter for worry
and publicity, until the exotic "Vega" was chosen. The car
was first described, and advertised, under a "code name,"
"XP-887." By early 1970, the business press speculated that
GM executives were divided over how to name the prodi-
gious new car—with one corporate faction, concerned about
brand identification, favoring the names "GM-ini,"
"G-Mini," or "Jiminy." Finally, in April 1970, the car was
baptized—in skywriting over downtown Detroit, "Chevrolet Names It Vega 2300." The Vega engine was meanwhile displayed at the 1970 New York Auto Show, on a
pillar draped with black velvet. Advertisements began to
appear in the spring: "Coming Soon: the Little Car That
Does Everything Well. Everything? Everything. . . ." Chevrolet publicists made their ambitions clear: "By the time it
actually goes on sale, we want this totally new car to be as
familiar to Americans as a member of their own family."

The Vega marketing campaign was extraordinary not
only for its scope and complexity, but also because of the
unprecedentedly portentous introspection that accompanied
it. Chevrolet announced that Vega advertisements would
"discuss the car's underlying philosophy." DeLorean of

Chevrolet complained, in an article about the Vega, that although "there's still a certain adventurous element in our social scheme . . . a lot of people just don't want the new thing, either in home appliances or in automobiles or in anything else." GM's "program of scientific market analysis" revealed that "the small car concept is more than just a matter of size. . . . What it really means is a new way of looking at transportation. . . ." In these soul-searchings, GM seemed to be asking more and more speculative questions: What is a small car? What are the hopes for auto salesmanship? How will U.S. automobiles change? What is a second car? What, in effect, is the future of the consuming family?

The modernity of the Vega, and of Vega philosophy, was reflected in the language of GM publicity. Early advertisements featured small drawings of the new car, and no photographs. Sentences were short and colloquial. Safety was mentioned, with economy, reliability, and serviceability. At the 1970 New York Auto Show, the new Vega engine had been displayed in the Chevrolet exhibition, near a show of new Chevrolet colors (which included, in an ironic reversal of Henry Ford's offer of a car any color so long as it was black, the color "tuxedo black") , and next to something described as a "Glen Campbell Camaro centerpiece which accents an open cockpit effect with a western-like interior of saddle vinyl and an exterior of greenish black pearlescent paint." Compared to this sort of extravagance, the Vega received a strikingly soft sell, a Volkswagen-like sell, for "modern" consumers: as *Motor Trend* magazine wrote when it chose the Vega as its 1971 "Car of the Year," Vega marketing was part of a move away from "what had come to be almost automotive parody of the pseudo-Gothic age in American architecture."

GM's Vega investigations, in all this modernity, were addressed to the sobering but well-established problems of the auto market. They recognized the two main, troublesome objectives of saturation marketing—altering (upgrading) the product, and altering (expanding) the total market for the product—and addressed the Vega to the second objective. This endeavor, and the attempt to make American families and American drivers buy two or more cars, has preoccupied the auto industry for at least fifteen years. The magazine *Sports Car Graphic,* in a fulsome account of the Vega's development, revealed that Detroit marketing divisions divide automobiles into two categories, Traditional and Contemporary. Traditional cars are six-passenger, four-door sedans, "conventional in concept" and "relegated to family use." All other cars, notably the Vega, are "new in concept" and Contemporary. They amount to more than half the total auto market, and are intended for multicar families, multicar drivers, and for households without conventional families.

"Contemporary" marketing first flourished in the early 1960s, when around 90 percent of all American households owned at least one car. Alfred Sloan himself, as an eighty-five-year-old consultant strategist, observed GM's development of the Contemporary car. The late 1950s and early 1960s, he wrote, "saw the most dramatic change in the car market since the 1920s . . . when the Model T came to an end, and the upgrading of cars began." From the early days of multicar marketing, automotive theorists were undecided about the potential appeal of the new cars: in the 1960s the auto companies investigated and sold an indiscriminate variety of cheap cars, foreign cars, women's cars, specialty cars, sporty cars, youth cars, cars which Sloan described as "pleasure" or "vacation" cars, or "special cars at higher prices." This change towards Contemporaneity was summarized for Sloan in the aphorism of a modern GM president: "Our object is not only a car for every purse and purpose but, you might say, a car for every purse, purpose, and person."

Most of the automotive introspection which greeted the Vega concerned the philosophy of the multicar family. The role of the second car appeared as a study in family psychology: Was the new car for mothers, or for teen-age children? Was it for childless couples? Or for single working women? Contemporary marketing became a problem of social organization—how was the Vega to be inserted into the crevices of the family group? One auto magazine designated the Vega and other subcompacts as suitable for schoolgirls and secretaries. DeLorean of Chevrolet pronounced that many small-car buyers, perhaps unmarried or childless, "look for a car that represents their life style—which is practical, fun-loving, simple, and outgoing." Yet, writing in *Motor Trend,* he argued for a more traditional, or Traditional, vision of the automotive family: "When going from New York to Los Angeles, there's nothing like a big car, for the comfort and ability to move around and carry the two sets of golf clubs and enough baggage for the whole family." *Sports Car Graphic* explained the distinction between Traditional and Contemporary cars in an even more contemplative discussion of the sociology of the Vega. Like De-Lorean, it described consumer enthusiasm for Contemporary cars as a matter of "changing life styles," in the most momentous sense: "At one time, family unity was most important in this country.... Today, family ties have loosened. There is no dramatic reason for having a large automobile."

The result of these investigations was an all-purpose Contemporary car, a mutation with traits borrowed from decades of past marketing. All the changes noted by De-Lorean became part of a giant statistical survey. The corporation's "national probability study" did not confine its investigations to the appeal of foreign cars. The project was based on interviews with 8,600 consumers, 400 Chevrolet dealers, and 600 "key Chevrolet wholesale personnel," and on more informal meetings at "space clinics" and "space utilization clinics"; it provided information for an undisclosed number of Vega "study groups," such as the Product Assurance Group, the Engine Group, and the Pleasability Group. The apparent purpose of the operation was to find out why anyone had ever bought a Contemporary car. The qualities associated with successful second cars, such as, perhaps, sportiness, smallness, convenience, exoticness, foreignness, modernity, or extraversion were digested by GM's computers—which then created the Vega. Even the human engineers working on the Vega project seemed to accept the principle of "probability" design: the Vega chief engineer was quoted as remarking, "We think we've achieved a pretty good compromise here," between the fuel economy of a Volkswagen and the performance of a (Ford) Maverick. The Vega seemed to have a slight resemblance to every second car that every ("statistically significant") section of the population had ever liked.... For the American automotive press, this lack of spontaneity was the Vega's gravest defect: according to one journal the Vega was engineered within an inch of its life, another called it a "numbers car," and a third pronounced that the Vega looked as if it had been designed by a computer.

(The last famous "numbers" car was the Ford Edsel—which was to the upgraded family sedan of the 1950s what the Vega was to the modern second car. As awkward automotive ideals, the two cars had much in common. Edsels were intended for upwardly mobile families, trading from modest to elaborate cars. Like the Vega, the Edsel was portentously philosophical: in the "Fate of the Edsel" John Brooks quotes Ford's Edsel presentation in the summer of 1957: "One of the great aspects of this whole Edsel program is the philosophy of product and merchandising behind it. . . . Never again will we [who have been a part of it] be associated with anything as gigantic and full of meaning as this particular program." Edsels, like Vegas, were launched with a long and expensive prenatal campaign, on the theme of "peek and tell." Like Vegas, they were "Younger: appealing to spirited but responsible adventurers," with "Family: not exclusively masculine; a wholesome 'good' role." And, like Vegas, they were troubled by defects of design and production—even to the extent that the dashboards of both cars tended to burst alarmingly into flames. The main difference between the two cars was, of course, that the Edsel, introduced at the beginning of a cyclical depression in the auto economy, was a spectacular failure, and the Vega a modest success: 323,000 people bought Vegas in 1971, and 307,000 in 1972—although it is not recorded whether these people were male or female, or young in life style, or whether they bought Vegas instead of larger, more expensive cars.)

Vega selling reflected the car's complicated origins. The problems of stimulating demand for second cars had no easy solution. Even in their Contemporary ventures, auto strategists remained fixed on the lavish patterns of past marketing. The earliest Vegas boasted a bold variety of contradictory qualities. The Edsel had been, for Ford, "a different car in every respect, yet it [had] an element of conservatism which would give it maximum appeal"; even as a Contemporary car, the Vega had residual characteristics of the Traditional, upgraded sedan. One Vega advertisement featured the headline *Little, But Big.* " The car was "a lot bigger than its size would indicate"—or, as DeLorean of Chevrolet put it, with his customary thoughtfulness, "Automotive size, including smaller size, refers to a concept and not merely to physical facts."

Cheap But Luxurious. The Vega was economical, modestly priced, even "stingy"—and could become attractively opulent: "The inside isn't fancy. But it sure isn't plain."

Adventurous But Substantial. The car was "amazingly peppy," and suitable for the open road: "Why, a young dentist wrote to tell us that he drove coast to coast with all his worldly possessions stacked inside his Hatchback." Yet the Vega also boasted a more Traditional appeal, the sort of solidity which drivers might have found in a family sedan of the middle 1950s: "You'll be able to tell the minute you see it that this is a car of substance. You'll be able to tell better by sitting in it, slamming its doors, pounding its fenders, revving its engines, feeling its power and grip on the road."

Womanlike But Manly. GM tried to locate the Vega quite precisely within the two-car family. The Vega sedan was a woman's car. Vega advertisements implied that when the man of a household chooses a Traditional car, the woman will skittishly demand a Vega. *Automotive News* published a guide to "How to Pitch Subcompacts to Today's Women": it pointed out that women were the "prime market" for cars like the Vega, and urged dealers to remember that "Mama probably will decide where her young drivers will go for their first cars." Meanwhile, the Vega, the "Little Car That Does Everything Well," was overequipped even in its gender. The basic Vega sedan was for wives; the Vega fastback coupe hatchback GT had *machismo* appeal. *Motor Trend* road-tested the Vega GT and found it "sporty," attractively adrenalin-inducing, and styled with "a lot of Camaro and a dash of Maverick in the rear." (Cars like Camaros and Mustangs, "muscle units," "high performance units," or "super cars," sold brilliantly in the middle to late 1960s, particularly to single men and to rich husbands.)

Old But Young. The Vega was Traditional. It was "every inch a Chevrolet and proud of it." But it had special appeal for younger American generations. DeLorean expressed the hope that the Vega would appeal to the youth market, schoolgirls and schoolboys, including "a significant number of college students." The Vega Pleasability Group employed young engineers—called "Pleasability Engineers"—whom Chevrolet public relations officers described as "tuned in to youth."

GM's rhetoric about the Vega accurately identified the problems of modern second-car marketing. Yet much of the Vega sales campaign could have been designed thirty-five or fifteen years ago. The selling of the upgraded Vega recalled the 1930s, while the car's Contemporary appeal was based on the salesmanship of the late 1950s, with the accumulated seductiveness of second cars throughout the 1960s. The new "life style" of Vega publicity, the public soul-searching of high company executives, the years which Chevrolet's research and motivation teams spent in analyzing U.S. auto stagnation, all added up to an expensive exercise in nostalgia.

The Vega probability study seemed to sum up this sense of stagnation: a massive analysis of past attitudes, inert with information, whose central instructions scanned again and again the unanswerable troubles of the automotive family. Yet the problems of automotive selling, as shown in the Vega project, go even beyond such inertia. Auto managers faced not only a choice between different techniques of marketing and promotion, but also a long and historical crisis of auto demand. Three months before the Vega was launched, Richard Gerstenberg, now chairman of GM, and then a rising financial executive, delivered a somber address to the World Advertising Forum in New York. His subject was the Crisis in Communications, and he argued that communications were now more than ever an art, that "we have to show that without profit there can be no progress": "In the dictionary sense, a crisis means a moment for decision. I think the business community—at least in America—has come to such a moment." The sort of decision that auto executives made, in the marketing of Vegas and other modern cars, required more than an "art of communications," and went beyond tactical considerations of spontaneity or eclecticism, of appeals to the old or to the young, of location in cyclical auto fluctuations—to questions about why, or whether, Americans would buy more family cars, in a congested national market. Auto saturation is not simply a matter of statistics. About 10 million passenger cars are sold each year in the United States (of which more than a million are foreign-made, while at least another million are sold not to consumers but to government agencies, corporate fleet operators, auto rental companies). As shown in the development of Sloanist selling, the U.S. auto market has already passed several apparently plausible limits in the ratio of cars to families, and of cars to drivers; the most euphoric managers of the 1940s and 1950s expected an insignificant future for the multicar family. Yet market saturation is determined by consumer attitudes, by the social context and convenience of the products offered. Almost all automobiles are bought as replacements for older cars—most in the system of installment selling, where cars are bought on credit and traded in after two or three years. While this cycle made possible past automotive growth, it is also peculiarly vulnerable to changes in spending if consumers decide to keep their old cars longer or to trade down to cheaper cars. Modern automobiles, including the Vega, face problems of familiarity, of unreliability in advertising, pricing, and safety, of apparent consumer distaste for Sloanist policies. They face further problems of social convenience, as supporting and operating an automobile becomes ever more frustrating. These problems could indicate the likely human limit to auto saturation: it is such limits which the Vega project can help to explain—and the relationship between these limitations and the past excesses of auto selling.

. . .

In 1947, *Fortune* published an "issue dedicated to American Selling." The magazine wrote enthusiastically of the advertising industry, and of J. Walter Thompson, but reserved its most admiring comment for the "ubiquitous Buick": it dated the ascendance of the Buick from 1936, when "Buick [advertising] copy ceased to list all the nuts and bolts in the product and started saying things like 'Dressed for a Party—Powered for a Thrill.'" Few contemporary business journals are sufficiently ingenuous or uncynical to offer a hymn to American selling, but if such a discussion were possible, advanced business comment would be likely to ignore or deprecate automotive marketing. The modern auto market, which is the most elaborate of all markets, in America or in the history of world selling, is also the market most troubled by consumer criticism, and by business disapproval.

One reason for present automotive dissatisfaction is simply the overdevelopment of auto sales techniques, as refined during the nearly forty years of marketing since Buick's advertising effort of the mid-1930s. Yet discontent reaches past modes of selling. Auto sales are supported by a complex arrangement of social necessity: most people in America, however impervious they may be to auto persuasion, need an automobile in order to get to work, or to school, or to a store. (Beyond this most powerful convenience, automobiles still serve as a focus for national emotions, for freedom, solitude, even for suicide. Getting into a car and driving away is still a great American Way of Escape; driving to work is for many people a paramount opportunity to be alone; perhaps one in four of all American suicides is achieved in auto crashes, according to doctors in Houston who conducted "psychological autopsies" on people killed in auto crashes, and concluded that one in seven of all road deaths should properly be considered as a suicide.)

A major contradiction of the auto market is that automobiles are simultaneously necessary and exasperating. The country is organized around auto transportation: as Henry Ford wrote, "We have remade this country with automobiles." On the one hand, autos are comparable to housing or medical care, as requirements of social life; on the other hand, they are sold with the frivolous extravagance of detergents or deodorants. This callously established contrast can perhaps help to explain the resentment which characterizes modern auto purchasing. Automotive hyperbole is discovered everywhere. The incomprehensible but inflated pricing of autos and auto parts seems most intolerable when cars are necessities, and are also the largest item of most families' expenditure. It is peculiarly unacceptable that cars should break down repeatedly and unpredictably when they are required for so many daily routines, and that cars should be defective when they are so well placed to kill and to maim. These different reasons for resentment can explain some specific causes of automotive discontent, and some of the factors that contribute to auto saturation. Each of these disappointments is found in the case of the Vega—a normal car with normal troubles, but a car which, with its lavish and advanced advertising campaign, may perhaps have suggested intimations of modernity that it proved unable to support.

Exaggeration. The presentation of the Vega, as safe, re- liable, and economical, was designed to replace well- established fears with an unaccustomed confidence. But these expectations were soon destroyed. One attack came in a complaint by the Federal Trade Commission against GM and its advertising agency: as reported laconically by the *Wall Street Journal,* the Commission "alleges that GM used unfair practices in its 1971 ad claim that the Chevrolet Vega is the best-handling car ever built in the U.S." Other embarrassing boasts included an early advertisement de- scribing the Lordstown assembly line as "our highly auto- mated assembly line, which assures that every Vega will be built with an unequaled uniformity of quality." The Center for Auto Safety listed other inconsistencies in a letter to the chairman of GM: "Dear Mr. Gerstenberg, We are writing in regard to 'the little car that does everything well'—in- cluding bursting into flames, accelerating uncontrollably, and losing its rear wheels: General Motors' Chevrolet Vega." The Center wrote that it received letters of com- plaint from Vega owners "at a shockingly rapid" and "ever- increasing" rate; many hundreds of owners felt that they had been misled by Vega advertising, and, specifically, by claims that the Vega was economical, easy to service, and gave good gas mileage.

The "modern" Vega was perhaps an extreme case in its capacity for inspiring and then dashing consumer expecta- tions. Yet the pattern of exaggeration and disappointment is found throughout auto selling. As with the Vega, the most bitter disappointments concern safety: J. Z. De- Lorean, who as head of Chevrolet presided over the Vega presentation, has been reported as proclaiming that "every defect, each recall, only diminishes the credibility of whatever amount of advertising we do," while poor quality "has already resulted in seriously declining owner-loyalty to our products and reduced credibility of our promises to do better next time." Other inadequacies appear in less lethal situations. The FTC analysis of auto advertising demanded company documentation for such claims as that Ford LTDs were quieter than "some of the world's most expensive cars," and that the Vega was the "best-handling passenger car ever built in the U.S." GM submitted a biography of the automotive journalist who first made the extravagant claim about Vega handling; Ford submitted the results of two six-year-old tests, and of a third test comparing a 1971 Ford with a 1970 Mercedes. According to the *Wall Street Journal*, Ford's third test was "meaningless" for "statisticians": " 'That wasn't the point of the ad,' a Ford spokesman says, when asked [by the *Wall Street Journal* reporter] about the ad's validity. 'We just wanted to show a rich-looking guy with a well-maintained, expensive car, let him ride in a Ford and show how impressed he was with its quietness.' The quietness is really proven, he says, by a different test that demonstrates it's much quieter inside the '71 LTD than outside it. That test doesn't compare the LTD with any other vehicle."

This unreliability of auto advertising is in part a consequence of past marketing. Auto public relations, although emulated in thousands of other consumer markets, now seem familiar and predictable; the president of American Motors warned, on an occasion as festive as the dinner and ball preceding the 1972 New York Auto Show, that business has encouraged the militancy of the modern consumer:

"In our competitive efforts to win his attention, we too often built up his expectations to unrealistic levels and must share the blame when he is disappointed. There is no doubt that promotional excesses have come back to haunt us and we are paying the price for these indiscretions." The basic claim of upgraded marketing, about the newness of new-model cars, is itself exaggerated. The Vega was New, yet Old. Few American cars are new in more than appearance: the general pattern of auto inertia, where corporations produce technologically unadventurous cars, by a technologically conventional process, itself affects the credibility of auto publicity.

Advertising exaggeration, as in the case of the Vega, may contribute to the troubles of a particular car; it is certainly an important cause of modern discontent with automobiles and with the paraphernalia of auto selling. *Fortune* recently published a business profile of a Cleveland Ford dealer, which it introduced in the most strikingly gloomy language (far from the optimism of the 1947 special issue on American selling): "By a wide margin, automobile dealers are the businessmen Americans distrust most. Used-car dealers have long been popular targets for suspicion and scorn (and wry jokes), but in recent years public antipathy has engulfed new car dealers as well. According to a recent Gallup poll, Americans have five times as much confidence in an undertaker, and even three times as much confidence in a plumber, as they do in a car dealer." This distrust is in part a result of the increasingly contemptuous familiarity of autos and auto advertising; *Fortune* talked to a salesman who had worked at the Cleveland dealership since 1936, and who said, "It used to be a big thing to buy a car. People would dress up. The ladies would wear white gloves and the men would have on ties and suits. It isn't like that anymore."

Pricing. The vexed problems of auto pricing were particularly acute in the case of the Vega. Vegas were presented as cheap and economical, yet they always suggested luxury. Even the earliest Vegas were more expensive than their rivals, the Pintos and the simpler Toyotas and Volkswagens—in obedience, apparently, to Alfred Sloan's precept, laid down in 1921, "We proposed in general that GM should place its cars at the top of each price range." Since the decline of the Model T Ford, when "the upgrading of cars began," the U.S. auto corporations have rejected cheap cars. The major object of Sloanist marketing was to make cars more expensive; even when they sold Contemporary or second cars, the companies were reluctant to offer bare automobiles, which might encourage a regrettably ascetic consumer mood.

Vegas were the result of some twenty-five years of corporate planning for a cheap but nonascetic car—planning which resulted by 1959 in the Chevrolet Corvair, and by 1970 in the Vega. GM's strategic attitude to such a car was explained by the corporation in 1958. Harlow H. Curtice, the president of GM, appeared before the Kefauver Committee hearings on Administered Prices in the Automobile Industry. He was questioned by the committee about GM's efforts to combat the menace of foreign cars, and about the import of German Opels. Curtice's language is reproduced as it appears in the official transcript of the hearings:

SENATOR O'MAHONEY: Do you plan to build a small car here in the U.S. to compete with imported small cars?
CURTICE: For over the years that has been a subject that we have constantly studied. Thus far it has not been practical from the standpoint of the economics to offer the small car, on the basis that because you take the value out so much more rapidly than you can take the cost out.

Curtice's fairly cryptic remarks seem to imply that auto manufacturers have greater freedom to determine "value," as measured by price, when they sell large expensive cars than when they sell small, cheap cars; and that the manufacturers have little freedom to determine the "costs" of auto production. Consumers probably mind less about prices when they are buying expensive cars than when they are buying economy cars, and the auto corporations charge wildly different prices for the most superficially distinguishable cars. Many American cars are made out of much the same pieces, and are put together in more or less the same way. Large cars use more metals and other raw materials than small cars, and expensive cars have more extra equipment added during the assembly process. Yet the progress of a car down a moving assembly line, as doors and windows and radios and engines are added, is largely the same for different kinds of cars.

According to the principles of Sloanist marketing, cheap cars must become more expensive year by year (while small cars should, usually, become larger). The small, cheap Chevrolet Corvair appeared in 1959; after 1960, new Corvairs were more and more expensive, and after 1964 they were longer. Vegas, originally the most expensive of American subcompact cars, experienced a similar upgrading. The cars were available from the start in four different models, sedan, "hatchback coupe," station wagon, and panel truck; they could be equipped with a lavish selection of optional extras, from large engines to air conditioners to oval tires to special interior trim. (The corporation also investigated the possibility of offering further Vega models. By 1972, according to *Motor Trend,* "Chevrolet [had] put together or cut out just about every type of variation on Vega you could imagine. An El Camino-type Vega, V8 Vega, sunroof Vega, super-plush Vega, turbo-Vega, convertible Vega, and a four-door Vega . . . all concocted to see if it will sell. The 4-wheel-drive Vega Snowbird is something else again.")

The average Vega's load of accessories increased from 1970 to 1971, and again from 1971 to 1972. By the summer of 1972 most Vegas went on sale with costly options: according to workers at the Lordstown factory, few came off the line with less than several hundred dollars' worth of extra equipment. One optimistic Wall Street auto analyst saw this sort of compulsory upgrading as central to "GM's strategy in the 1973 model year." Cheap cars were replaced with more expensive models: "In effect, we have the consumer being forced to upgrade his purchases." Vega options seemed to have a particularly hopeful future. The analyst looked at rates of installation of air conditioning: "The Vega is (comparatively) low at 22.4 percent," and "far from saturation." "I think," he said, "there is great potential for increasing option installation rates on the low-end cars."

Pricing practice is perhaps the most incomprehensible

and unpopular aspect of all auto selling. This unpopularity
goes beyond the price and availability of different options,
and beyond even the general inflation of auto prices. In its
article about the Cleveland Ford dealer, *Fortune* wrote that
"nothing about the automobile arouses more confusion and
distrust than the way in which it is priced": it quotes the
somber opinion of the Cleveland dealer: "I don't believe
that more than 15 percent of the new-car buyers are at
peace with themselves on the way home, and think they got
a good deal. That's the tragedy of this business."

Auto prices are determined by the most dense tangle of
advertised or list prices, trade-in values on old cars, dis-
counts, seasonal allowances, dealer profits and costs, prepa-
ration charges, option prices. Of all consumer markets, the
auto market is the darkest and most secret—where in a
grotesque exaggeration of free enterprise every price is
mysterious, and every sale a "deal." The General Motors
Acceptance Corporation finance company boasts that "We
Uncomplicate Things," but auto deals are among the most
complex of all retail transactions. Serious consumers must
study and bargain: *The New York Times*, noting that list
prices are set above expected prices, and that, according to
an FTC study, only 18 out of a hundred car buyers pay close
to the list price, recommends that consumers should buy
cars at the end of a month, when dealers are trying to fill
their incentive quotas, and should bargain on the basis of
calculations about the cost of cars to dealers, which, for full-
size cars, might be 78 percent of the list price less transportation costs.

The mystification of auto pricing is a most evident cause
of present auto dissatisfaction—and like other such causes

it has a basis in the auto industry's historical situation. Automobiles, although lavishly expensive relative to family spending, are sold at retail in an atmosphere of complexity that would be unacceptable for the cheapest groceries or cosmetics: the reason for this can be found in the past development of Sloanist marketing, which concealed its annual upgrading in an elaborate pricing system. Annual "improvements" and inflation, and the upgrading of options, are perceptible to the consumer only through a tangle of bargains and deals. For Alfred Sloan, the transformation of the auto market in the 1920s was made possible by "installment selling" and by the "used-car trade-in" (and also by the "closed body," the "annual model," and by "improved roads"). In 1925, Sloan wrote, "it was reasonable to assume that consumers would lift their sights to higher levels of quality. Installment selling, we thought, would stimulate this trend." Credit purchasing made possible the system of franchised dealerships, in which, as Sloan put it, "everyone should hold up his end of the relationship and be rewarded accordingly," and where the auto manufacturers' "contact" is "not [with] the customer," but with the dealer, and with "the public as a whole."

Auto dealers are the immediate focus for consumer resentment, yet they are sometimes just as much as consumers the victims of the auto pricing "system." The structure of auto prices, from factory to showroom, is based on the harshest principles of internal competition. Dealers compete to fulfill manufacturers' objectives, under the threat of sanctions and the promise of incentives. The dealers in turn offer incentives to their own salesmen, who operate under the constant pressure of bonuses, exhortations, mutual rivalry. This automotive survival of the fittest amounts to a complex system of buck-passing, from the manufacturers to the dealers to the salesmen. Thousands of little bargains add up to a deal—while for the participants, for dealers, salesmen, and most of all for consumers, the entire process assumes the force of objective and inscrutable necessity.

(The very back-slapping of the auto showroom can seem to possess an independent existence, as shown in the researches of a Chicago business economist named Allen F. Jung. Jung investigated the ways in which consumer credulity affects auto economics: according to an academic expert on the auto industry, "Jung first experimented with different approaches to the dealer, which involved timid-unknowledgeable, medium-knowledgeable, and forthright-knowledgeable approaches." My own, recent, experiment involved an ambiguously knowledgeable approach to a Chevrolet dealer in New York City, the Midtown Chevrolet operation, which is owned by GM. I found out what different Vegas cost, and that the transportation charge for Vegas was $54, although the relationship ("what you get for a little extra") between the special handling package, which cost $129 and improved the car's ride, and the GT package, which for $313 improved the ride and the car's appearance, remained puzzling. The dealership showroom was decorated with a poster that seemed to epitomize the hopes of Vega domesticity: "You're not going to believe this," it said, showing the Smith family from Summerville, South Carolina, a mother, father, two sons and a daughter, each of whom, for idiosyncratic reasons, owned a Chevrolet Vega. The salesman I spoke with told me, spontaneously, that "Cars today are made by the hand of man, and not by the hand of God." I asked him about the Vega recalls, and he said, "That was last year." (I visited the dealership early in 1973.) He spoke approvingly of the recall procedure, saying "It's the best thing that's ever happened," and that "otherwise, the [defective] cars would be driving around." Rolls-Royces had been recalled, he continued, adding, in a proud rating of corporate power, that "We recalled four million cars this year, Ford recalled three million, and Chrysler two million.")

Reliability. Of all automotive troubles, troubles with product safety and reliability provide the most public focus for consumer discontent. The Center for Auto Safety has told the dismal story of Vega reliability. In its letter to Mr. Gerstenberg of GM, it summarized consumer complaints about the Vega. People who had bought Vegas said that the three recalls of Vegas for safety defects had destroyed their faith in the car. They complained about the cars' brakes, which often vibrated and veered frighteningly, and about some Vega brakes that were more seriously deficient. They complained that the cars were difficult to start, and stalled dangerously in traffic. They complained about the Vega electrical system, which sometimes failed completely, and about the uncomfortable gearshift lever, which sometimes fell off. One Pennsylvania Vega owner wrote that his Vega leaked, and that "it's extremely difficult to drive home from work with FOUR INCHES of water surrounding your feet."

These failings were minor irritations compared to the defects for which Vegas were recalled. The first statutory recall was announced in April 1972, and involved 130,000

Vegas equipped with an optional 90-horsepower engine. A combination of deficiencies in the carburetor and the muffler could cause fires in the Vega gas tank; as an official letter from Chevrolet to Vega owners put it, "After the muffler has ruptured . . . fuel spillage" may occur, or "failure of the fuel line hoses," and "subsequent backfires then can ignite the spilled fuel and cause your Vega to catch fire." The second recall, announced in May 1972, involved 350,000 Vegas with standard 80-horsepower engines, and brought the number of Vegas recalled to 86 percent of total production—an inadequacy in a Vega idling mechanism could cause the car's accelerator pedal to jam while the car was moving. The third recall, announced in July 1972, involved 95 percent of all Vegas built before May 1972— some of the cars had a rear axle that was "a fraction of an inch" too short, so that a wheel might fall off.

Vega defects, with their promise of ruptured mufflers and jammed accelerators, led car owners far from the enticing simplicity of early advertisements. The recall procedure involved owners yet again in the complexities of the factory/dealer/customer relationship. Dealers were required to modify defective cars, yet sometimes found difficulty in obtaining the replacement parts they needed. Some dealers complained that the auto companies refused to cover the real cost of performing recall repairs, and ignored, for example, dealers' bookkeeping costs. Customers feared that when their cars were taken for free and mandated repairs, they would be charged for other repair jobs. They often faced weeks and months of delay—and meanwhile of driving to work or to school in possibly lethal cars.

The Vega's history is hardly exceptional. In 1971, the

auto industry staged 235 safety recalls, involving 9.4 million vehicles—there were about 110 million vehicles on the roads in America, and some cars, like Vegas in 1972, may have been recalled more than once. Few foreign or domestic cars are now innocent of recall. Even Cadillac succumbed, in 1972, with the calling in of 3,878 vehicles, including assorted ambulances and hearses. (Occasional ambulances were built with faulty rear axles.) Consumers can expect a full range of problems, in design, manufacturing, and finish. When they attempt auto repairs, they may face delays at least as arduous as those involved in the Vega recalls; most defective parts will need to be replaced rather than repaired, with spare parts sold to dealers and to the public at prices so inflated that it would cost some $6,400 to buy separately the parts for a $2,500 Ford Maverick.

Unreliability, of a more or less lethal sort, now seems a routine of the auto market. The Vega's faults were in fact relatively minor, and the cars have yet to develop a serious structural fault—unlike, for example, the otherwise comparable Chevrolet Corvair, whose instability was described by Ralph Nader in 1965. Until the recent refinement of the public recall procedure, Vega defects might have been ignored, or repaired at random. The consumer movement is itself in part responsible for consumer awareness of "minor" auto deficiencies—yet this normality of defectiveness in turn encourages further discontent.

The causes of auto unreliability have to do with the character of modern mass production, where complex products are manufactured in an atmosphere of unremitting cost efficiency. Many of the Vega's faults, for example, can be traced to the sort of corporate constraints which Ralph

Nader described in *Unsafe at Any Speed,* and which, according to Nader, shaped the development of the Corvair. Both Vegas and Corvairs were cheap cars, designed to compete with the Volkswagen. The Vega was GM's newest and most vaunted car since the Corvair: both cars were chosen as *Motor Trend*'s "Car of the Year." Nader described the creation of the Corvair in phrases that could apply to the Vega: "Cole and his associates were not in any mind merely to produce an American stereotype of the Volkswagen. This was to be a brand-new kind of car utilizing the lessons of past models and the advances of the latest automotive technology." Cole was head of Chevrolet in the 1950s and the main sponsor of the Corvair; by 1970 he was not only president of GM but also, reportedly, a senior corporate sponsor of the Vega. According to Nader, the Corvair's lethal instability was sanctioned by a failure of "initiative" on the part of company engineers, who were unable to overrule stylists and cost-efficiency experts. He describes the cost-cutting which characterized every stage of the Corvair's design and production; the Vega was developed with a similar determination to reduce production costs, by simplifying parts, saving materials, and by designing an easily assembled car—by, as the *Wall Street Journal* put it, "wring[ing] out" about $45 in labor costs for every Vega.

Many of the Vega's faults seem related to cost-cutting. In the first, "fire hazard," Vega recall, GM replaced some Vega mufflers with less "tolerant" mufflers, and its suppliers could presumably have used a stronger material in the first place. The second, "jammed accelerator," recall, was a straightforward design defect. According to the *Wall Street*

Journal, "GM's correction [was] an extra support device, aimed at preventing the bracket from failing. A GM spokesman said the bracket failure was unanticipated in the design of the car, and apparently is caused by engine resonance and vibration." The third, "short rear axle," recall was probably caused by a failure in manufacture and inspection procedures when the rear axles were made. Other Vega faults were the result of similar inspectional disorganization. *Car* magazine tested a Vega and found it unsatisfactory in the "most elementary aspects": Chevrolet engineers finally traced the car's faults to a management "assembly goof," for "due to a computer error, the car, which had automatic transmission, had been built with the front springs for the three-speed manual transmission." The veering tendency of Vega brakes, to take another example, was well known to GM before the Center for Auto Safety reported owners' complaints. Soon after the Vega was first introduced, one auto magazine described a Vega which, when braked hard, began "a violent dance," and another described a braking Vega which "shook, hopped, and started to swerve." As early as September 1970, *Motor Trend* had noted the Vega's "hairy left skid" when braking fast: it revealed that Chevrolet engineers knew about the problem, and had already controlled the veering "as much as possible."

These deficiencies are, perhaps, an expected consequence of corporate constraints, or of modern mass production. As defects of manufacturing organization and inspection, they may indicate a need for less complexity, less cost efficiency, and more human control, not only on the assembly line but throughout the productive process. They are, however, hardly the fault of Lordstown workers. Company executives sometimes imply that assembly workers are to blame for auto defects, as when DeLorean complained recently about product quality and workmanship, and, according to *The New York Times*, "cited labor disputes and accompanying charges of sabotage, singling out the Lordstown strike (of 1972)." Yet other production managers provide more plausible explanations: the head of the General Motors Assembly Division, and chief overseer of the Lordstown Vega plant, has told a newspaper reporter that "since 1966 only five percent of all our callbacks have been related to assembly." DeLorean's successor as head of Chevrolet says, abruptly, that "any manager who blames quality problems on his labor force had better start looking in the mirror." At Lordstown, at least the more serious of the Vega faults date from weeks or months before the cars reached workers on the final assembly line.

The dismal routines of auto unreliability reflect the auto industry's historical strategy of combining elaborate styling with cost-conscious production, its policy for pricing cars and car repair parts, its advertising exaggeration. And like these other causes, the auto-safety pattern appears peculiarly unsatisfactory in the context of automotive domination. It seems scarcely necessary to explain consumer discontent with unsafe cars; many different consumer products are unreliable, yet few have the power of life and death wielded by the family car. Few mass products sell for around one third of the median American family income, and few cost an average of $321 every time they are repaired. The auto market depends on social necessity, on the fact that people need automobiles in their daily lives: it is exactly this necessity that can explain the force of auto discontent. Auto owners, often entirely dependent on motor transportation, need reliable cars more than they need any but the most basic social services. There are few American consumers more understandably anxious than the Vega owner struggling to drive home from work ankle-deep in water, than the parent driving around town in an indispensable car which may or may not be eligible for a safety recall, and may or may not burst suddenly into flames.

Saturation. The many troubles of the Vega—the exaggerated advertising, the mysterious pricing, and the unsafe product—seem based on the historical situation of the auto market; these troubles can show how automotive discontent may itself affect the limits of auto selling. Even the Vega, a self-consciously modern car, was presented according to principles of marketing laid down in the youth of the auto age, and the inertia of Vega selling can help to explain the social context of auto saturation: it seems particularly fitting that the business that founded advanced American selling should be the modern industry most preoccupied with consumer hostility, and most alarmed by the prospect of market saturation.

As luxuries, automobiles now seem familiar and unexciting, decked with the coquetry of forty upgraded years. Even *Automotive News* perceives that "car buying always competes for spendable income with other products and services," and that "many motorists may come to the point where they decide . . . to buy a boat instead of the second or third car" (or a video tape recorder or a holiday cottage or an extra vacation). As necessities, cars may face even more serious problems. *Automotive News*'s reporter argues that "when the point is reached where drivers in urban areas must crawl along at 10 miles per hour and pay outrageous parking fees, much of [the automobile's] convenience is gone." "If the air quality in some cities deteriorates so badly that cars are banned from downtown and parking restrictions and disincentives come into play, motorists may balk at buying and driving," and may "decide to fly, take a bus or a train instead of driving." Automotive moderation can become a matter of convenience, at least for urban consumers, and for people who drive to work; families may forgo extra cars not because of innate capriciousness, but because such self-denial is made rational by the frustrations of congestion and morning traffic.

The auto market was sustained through its magnificent growth by governments that built highways for interstate travel, by developers who redesigned cities for the convenience of the automobile, by oil corporations that provided unlimited fuel at prices which ignored long-term social costs. To the auto consumer, such support was free, and invisible, and suburban development seemed part of an inevitable historical process. Yet the modern consumer must now pay the costs of this past license, as various authorities determine to reduce auto pollution and the congestion of cities. The burden of auto regulation will fall—and already falls—on consumers, who have in the past expected carefree and relatively taxfree motoring. Cars seem likely to lose not only their glamour as luxuries, but also their convenience as necessities of life, their freedom, their fiscal immunity—their already flawed appeal to American consumers.

Automotive saturation will eventually face limitations of space and energy: space is amply available, but not in the centers of manageable cities, or in, for example, central Los Angeles, where 60 percent of land is taken up by roads and parking space; energy is in less lavish supply, for an economy where almost a third of all petroleum consumed is burned in automobiles. Yet present automotive troubles suggest that the auto market is unlikely to approach these ultimate limits. It will be bounded, rather, by social constraints. Auto consumers, already discontented, will reject continued automotive growth before cities reach an apocalypse of immobility; governments will intervene to regulate the convenience of the automobile before Los Angeles chokes in smog, and before the gas pumps of America run dry.

These social and historical limits to the auto market provide the context of modern automotive troubles: discontent, in a market approaching social saturation, is only one manifestation of the historical decay of the automotive system. Any future fast and sustained expansion of auto sales will require a most radical transformation of automobiles and of urban transportation. Faced with the need for such a transformation, present auto adjustments will seem frivolous and inadequate, with their second-car refinements, their colloquial marketing, with the women's cars and adventurous cars and newly old cars of Vega selling.

The strategies of early Sloanism are at least partly responsible for modern automotive troubles, including the troubles of Vega marketing. Yet Sloanism developed with Fordist production technology, and the two foundations of auto policy remain interdependent. It will become clear from the history of the Lordstown Vega factories that Fordism has a relation to troubles of auto technology and auto workers' discontent similar to that of Sloanism to the Vega's marketing problems. Even beyond this resemblance, the two auto strategies are related, as market upgrading shapes the dismal history of mass production. Most important of all, the general consumer discontent with automobiles will itself seem to affect auto workers' attitudes.

Alfred Sloan described the development of GM styling by explaining that in the early 1920s the corporation employed "two kinds of engineers—one in product and the other in production—in a certain relation of tension which necessarily affected the design of the automobile. The production engineer's problems in creating techniques for mass production often caused him to want to hold up design changes in the product." But by the mid-1920s, the production engineer lost power to the product engineer, and the product engineer to the stylist: "The product engineer had begun to feel the influence of the sales people. He then began to yield to market considerations. . . . Now he devotes much of his skill to solving the problems created by the stylist." It remains true that corporate emphasis on styling has inhibited changes in mass production—and that this emphasis has even prevented major alteration in auto design. Sloan himself admitted, in the 1960s, that "we have today basically the same kind of machine that was created in the first twenty years of the industry"; many less basic auto improvements, such as automatic transmission, power steering, and synchromesh gears were developed before 1940.

This inertia of auto engineering was a result of the corporate preoccupation with presentation, shown in the Vega project, and in the development of other cars, such as Edsels and Corvairs. Many of the productive reorganizations used at Lordstown, including even the mechanical welding performed by Unimate robots, were based on principles laid down by Henry Ford; GM has announced recently the development of a "new" energy-absorbing bumper, yet some Pierce-Arrow automobiles built in the 1920s had pneumatic compressible bumpers, and the *Wall Street Journal* reports that auto industry engineers are now to be seen at the Henry Ford Museum in Dearborn, Michigan, photographing fifty-year-old pneumatic and hydraulic bumpers. Fordism and Sloanism together create a depressing pattern of corporate timidity, where conventional but elaborately styled cars are produced by conventional but elaborate processes—a pattern which will become most clear in the Lordstown developments.

Auto workers' discontent, as shown in Lordstown, is not caused simply by Fordist technology. Beyond problems of engineering, modern automotive troubles involve social dissatisfaction with automobiles, and this dissatisfaction can provide an appropriate introduction to Lordstown production. The auto abuses responsible for the historical congestion of the auto market seem, perhaps, particularly intolerable to people who make automobiles. The Lordstown workers whom I talked with complained about the pace of production and the inhumanity of management—but also about the disappointments of the Vega. One man, who said that "we don't see any $2,100 Vegas going off the line any more," told me that in his opinion GM had "no intent [for the Vega] to be competitive with the Volkswagen," that the corporation operated according to a five-year projection, with the "intention to make the Vega more expensive," that "like a Camaro . . . in a few years' time this car is going to be as expensive as a medium-size car." The same worker estimated that Vega bumpers cost a tiny fraction of the selling price of repair bumpers; he asked, "Who ever heard of an American car going a year without repairs or parts?" and said that if Rolls-Royce really offered a lifetime of free service, "a worker would be better off buying a Rolls-Royce." Many other workers talked about problems of auto safety and reliability. A woman worker in the Lordstown truck plant described her resentment when a "bad truck" goes by; she has too much work to do, but tries anyway to correct the truck's faults: "I should ship it, instead of busting myself to sort it out." A final comment on auto popularity comes from another woman worker at Lordstown: she told me that she had bought a Buick, a GM car—but now that she'd worked at Lordstown, "I would never buy a Chevy."

4

Auto Production: Lordstown

At Lordstown, GM prepared for the Vega the most expensive and technologically most ambitious factory in modern auto history. Lordstown efficiency was extolled in early Vega advertisements, and became essential to the presentation of Vegas as competitive with Toyotas and Volkswagens. Yet even the Lordstown investment was based on pure Fordism, as practiced in the days when eager young time-study engineers planned a new factory at Highland Park. Management attitudes were similarly fixed on past hopes. After the famous strike in 1972, over working conditions, Lordstown became a world center of worker alienation, and, for the business press, of a "Lordstown syndrome": the history of Lordstown can help to explain not only the disappointments of the Vega, but also the real context of auto workers' discontent, and of present auto troubles.

Automotive inertia is even more inexorable in production

than in selling. In the case of the Vega, the power of Fordism, as of Sloanism, was irresistible to General Motors. Like Vega selling, Lordstown mass production was organized according to forty-year-old industrial principles. Assembly technology suited early auto selling, and the two strategies developed together: modern cars, including Vegas, are sold with many options and additions; they are produced on moving assembly lines where each part is added quickly and dexterously; their elaborate assembling uses unskilled and minutely regulated work. The factory arrangements about which Lordstown workers complain are, as much as the troubles of auto marketing, a consequence of the auto industry's general immobility.

As GM's major model for future efficiency, the Lordstown Vega assembly factory was described in eager and uncharacteristic detail. Enthusiastic company executives explained the organization and technology of the new factory—even after the 1972 strike visitors who joined public tours of Lordstown were told that the Vega assembly line was the "fastest in the world" and "very automated." GM's own descriptions of the Lordstown factories can show how Fordist ideas are applied in the modern auto business: the implications of such technological dependency are shown in the history of the factory and its labor troubles, and in the things that people who work there say. This chapter will look at the Lordstown developments. The next will examine GM's version of the 1972 strike, according to which the sort of discontent found at Lordstown was inevitable, expected, and occurs at many other GM factories across America. It will show that Lordstown conditions of work are typical of other auto operations; that automotive production is determined by the mechanical necessities of auto technology and auto design, and that changes in assembly technology would require changes in auto selling and organization; that old patterns of production also shape management attitudes towards work, change, and new investment, as dread and inertia spread through the hierarchies of the auto business.

The Lordstown Vega factory began operating in June 1970, to rapturous business acclamation. The factory was not new, but renovated, at a cost of some hundreds of millions of dollars. Since 1966, GM had built Chevrolets at Lordstown, in the low-grade farmland between Pittsburgh and Cleveland; and from the earliest days the Lordstown work force was one of the youngest at any GM plant. By 1970, there were four factories in the Lordstown complex: Chevrolet auto assembly, Fisher body assembly, a new stamping plant, designed by a computer, and a new Chevrolet truck plant. The Chevrolet assembly plant had been redesigned, in accordance with what GM called the "entirely new concept of [Vega] assembly"—people who worked at the old Lordstown plant said that secretive GM engineers appeared at the factory in March 1970, "tearing the whole insides out and ripping up the line," even before the last of the Chevrolet Impalas were assembled.

By midsummer 1970, GM was ready to invite visitors to its new, improved Lordstown factories. Early Vega publicity emphasized the manufacture of the new, competitive car, at its new, competitive factory, and most early reactions were suitably awestruck. GM's labor-saving assembly techniques attracted national attention, as the corporation lamented the high level of U.S. wage rates. "Stomping the Beetle?" the *Wall Street Journal* asked from Lordstown, and announced that "GM resorts to aggressive automation to pare construction costs of mini-car . . . [and hopes to] be able to wring about 10 percent out of the normal labor costs of producing an automobile." Company executives suggested that the high quality of Vegas was made possible by Lordstown assembly efficiency: J. Z. DeLorean of Chevrolet described Vega "quality control," and pronounced in September 1970 that "the high level of enthusiasm among employees at the Lordstown plant is producing craftsmanship to challenge any auto maker in the world."

Corporate pride increased throughout the first year of Vega sales. The Lordstown project was, it seemed, of critical importance not only for the Vega but also for GM's entire campaign to increase productivity. The cover of the 1970 GM Annual Report showed a panorama of the Lordstown assembly plant, with two Vegas parked outside: the report also contained photographs of three men working on the Lordstown line, and of a "solid-state computerized tester" for Vegas.* As late as January 1972, Richard Gerstenberg, the chairman of GM, mentioned the Lords-

---

* GM's report covers provide a revealing chronology of the company's aspirations. 1969, two colored globes, with the legend that GM products are sold in 169 countries of the world: indicating a hope for profit through international expansion. 1970, Lordstown, and hopes for domestic productivity and second-car marketing. 1971, a tan Chevrolet and a turquoise Buick outside the GM "Emissions Research Center": the hope that traditional auto markets would be sustained by a new sort of obsolescence.

town operation as a major example of his company's efforts to increase worker productivity: "Every attempt was made [there] to design out costs in the assembly process." Earlier, an auto industry share analyst had summarized corporate hopes for Lordstown production, when he returned from a visit to the factory, "excited" about the prospects for reducing labor costs: "The essential point made was that the Vega line is a prototype, a schooling place for everybody in the GM system. . . . It is the wave of the future."

"Paradise Lost"

GM's presentation of Lordstown as the wave of the automotive future continued until February 1972—when workers at the Vega factories voted by a 97 percent majority to strike over working conditions. The strike vote came after months of struggle: a change in plant management, layoffs, a disciplinary crackdown, an increase in car defects, complaints by workers about the speeding up of monotonous assembly-line tasks, slowdowns, high absenteeism, repeated allegations by GM of worker sabotage. Workers claimed that supervisors authorized shipment of defective cars; the company claimed that workers attacked the paint, body, upholstery, and controls of the Vegas.

During the three-week strike which followed, and the months of subsequent resentment, GM executives restrained their public enthusiasm for Lordstown technology. But the distance between past expectations and present disaster was too great to be ignored, even by the most awestruck of previous visitors; and for the *Wall Street Journal* the

"Utopian" Lordstown factories had become nothing less than a "Paradise Lost," "fall[en] from grace." Public reactions to the strike were well described, six months later, by GM's director of labor relations. With heavy sarcasm, and a determination to "put the record straight," this executive declared that "the Lordstown chapter in the story of industrial life in the twentieth century will single out the Lordstown strike of 1972 as marking the explosion of youth and its rebellion against the management and union establishment." Once prototypes of efficiency, the Lordstown factories had now become prototypes of revolt. Commentators, from CBS and the U.S. Senate to *Motor Trend* and *Playboy*, converged on Lordstown; for one national journal the Vega plant was an "industrial Woodstock," where young workers acted out mysterious modern attitudes to work.

Even GM's labor relations executive was to admit after the Lordstown strike that "changes in the social environment are affecting our business in the area of motivation and behavior of employees," that GM employed, for example, more women, more blacks, and better-educated workers than in the past. But Lordstown workers and GM executives agreed that the famous 1972 strike had to do not only with social psychology but also with production issues, with layoffs, changed working conditions, and changed factory discipline. Most of these changes were the direct result of the same improvements and productive reorganizations that constituted GM's Lordstown "advances" in efficiency, and that made the new factory a "Paradise" for the business press. GM's own copious descriptions of Lordstown production may provide some explanation for worker discontent, and some idea of how advanced the Lordstown technology turned out to be.

Lordstown Fordism

From the days when Vegas were XP-887 experimental cars, and Lordstown workers built Chevrolet Impalas, GM's Lordstown policy was determined by Fordist exigencies: mechanization of jobs, reorganization of factory life, time, and space around unskilled work, and the modern auto imperative of cutting all costs, everywhere. Henry Ford's production had required the transfer of skills, and jobs, from workers to machines, and the "rationalization" of those jobs that could not be mechanized, and work was now so organized to be as precise, as predictable, and as machinelike as possible. In the Fordist "unity" of "men and machines," jobs followed the rhythms of mechanical production—as at Highland Park, so at Lordstown with its robots and computer controls.

The improvements of Lordstown production together forced a continuous reorganization of work—and their joint momentum can show to what extent Lordstown's designers had relied upon Fordist technology. The expensive Lordstown factories contained an unusually high concentration of mechanical innovations: for the present, cost-conscious auto industry, gloomy about future expansion, it often seems desirable to increase productivity in the cheapest possible ways, without new capital equipment; and, at GM, Mr. "Bookkeeper" Gerstenberg's main complaint about Lordstown was apparently that the corporation had "spent a terrific pile" of money on building the new factories. Yet even the most elaborate technology, such as the vaunted Lordstown robot welders, had progressed only modestly since the youth of mass production. The most ambitious of modern U.S. auto investments, Lordstown was still a product of Fordist practice.

Each of the three major "advances" built into the Lordstown factories—advances in mechanization, in factory planning (as helped by GM's computer designers), and in automatic controls and inspections—either was or could have been imagined by Henry Ford, and each increased the intensity and pace of unskilled work. Subsequent attempts to improve on the built-in and mechanical Lordstown innovations were a logical continuation of Fordist endeavor as refined by forty years of corporate cost efficiency. Henry Ford relied on his factory supervisors to discover when men and machines "wore out" or "needed to be replaced": for General Motors, determined managers could discover lost costs and idle moments overlooked by time-study engineers, and diligent foremen could find those inefficiencies that the managers had overlooked.

Mechanization, the first of the three categories of Lordstown innovation, has troubled the U.S. auto corporations for some fifty years. Now, as in the 1920s, automobiles are made out of thousands of metal and other parts, bolted or screwed or pushed or welded together: and now, as then, the assembling of the different parts is assumed to require some manual dexterity, some lowest human knack of visual coordination. Since the time of Henry Ford, the auto companies have tried to simplify their cars in such a way as to increase the number of assembly jobs which can be performed mechanically, while the development of auto marketing has required greater and greater elaboration in cars. But certain assembly jobs continue to demand an unskilled but barely mechanizable adaptability. People are still better than any but the most sophisticated, and *expensive,* automata at tightening bolts . . . or hanging wheels, or fixing steering columns, or, as two young women were doing at Lordstown a few months after the 1972 strike, jumping off and on the assembly line sliding grilles between the headlights of Vegas.

At Lordstown, the major effort at mechanization consisted of introducing the twenty-six "Unimate" robots which perform much of the welding on Vega bodies. (Before taking the public tour of the Vega factory, visitors are told that they will be particularly anxious to look out for the Unimates. During the tour, company guides cannot talk over the noise of the factory floor, and visitors ask one another whether each successive welding gun is in fact one of the famous robots. But when the group finally reaches them, the Unimates are unmistakable, white and contoured on a dreary iron line. They even move like science fiction automata—or, as one small boy who had joined the tour with his father and grandfather put it, "like little animals, nibbling the cars.")

The Lordstown robots in fact operate according to forty-year-old principles: in 1931 Henry Ford described the newly developed "automatic welding machine" which did the same job (of joining steel parts) as a human worker, and "went through the welding cycle automatically to completion." For Ford, the problem with such devices was their lack of adaptability, and GM's Lordstown experiences also illustrate some of the hazards of even the least adventurous assembly mechanization. As it turned out, the local management had almost as much trouble with its new machines as with its human "operators." One subsidiary machine, whose responsibility was to hand things to the Unimates, broke down repeatedly because of the "strain on key parts." Other new devices were even less dexterous. According to the *Wall Street Journal*, for example, the automatic spray guns that painted Vegas and remembered (or so it was hoped) whether the car to be painted was a coupe, a sedan, or a station wagon, developed a tendency to lose control, spraying paint into the air, the car windows, and assorted nearby holes.

Of these more or less efficient machines which replace unskilled labor, few improve factory working conditions, or change the character of the remaining jobs. DeLorean has written that the Lordstown Unimates "eliminate the obligation of the worker carrying a heavy welding gun around"—but also, and probably more candidly, that "one consideration is that we have mechanized many areas that would normally be areas of potential operator failure." Welding is comparatively easy to automate, and, besides, companies could not expect human workers to perform heavy welding one hundred times an hour. The introduction of automatic equipment sometimes actually creates new and more arduous jobs for unskilled workers. According to the head of the firm that manufactures them, Unimate robots are popular because "many 'subhuman' jobs are just not acceptable to workers today." Yet at Lordstown the Unimates themselves have human helpers—charged with the arguably subhuman job of preparing pieces of work, which they pass to the robot welders. As *Fortune* has described it, one of the "ironies" of automation is that machines often "take over the more skilled jobs, such as machining or welding, leaving the menial tasks for humans": "At Lordstown people pick up the sheet-metal panels and clamp them into position in the welding fixtures. At one time GM considered robotizing this job too. But the panels would have to be presented to the robot's clutching hands exactly the same way every time, and the machinery to accomplish this was judged prohibitively expensive." (The blind and clutching Unimates have an evident resemblance to the feeding machines in Chaplin's *Modern Times*. "Don't stop for lunch. Be ahead of your competitors.")

The second category of Lordstown innovation, factory planning, is similarly close to Fordist practice. Even more than the Lordstown attempts at mechanization, the planning of Lordstown production shows to what extent the modern auto corporations are dependent on old technology, and how that dependence affects the character of automotive work. The major principle of Lordstown production is the speed-up, as developed in the 1910s. One hundred and two cars pass along the final assembly line each hour; when the Lordstown line made Chevrolet Impalas it turned out sixty cars an hour, a normal rate, although some other factories now make as many as ninety cars each hour. Workers on the Vega line face a new car every thirty-six seconds— eight hundred Vegas in each eight-hour shift. Every change in factory arrangement supports the assembly speed-up: jobs, and the simplified Vegas, were redesigned to suit a thirty-six-second rhythm of production.

When GM engineers described the Lordstown project, they seemed particularly proud of their organizational achievements. One of their main ambitions in the project was to use "computer technology" to make each employee's job "easier to perform in a more precise way." It is cheaper to increase the precision and speed of production work than to replace workers with speedy (and perhaps clumsy) robots; and precise work, for auto engineers, usually means increased work. As the president of the Lordstown local union described it, to *The New York Times*, "That's the fastest line in the world. A guy has about forty seconds to do his job. The company does some figuring and they say, 'Look, we only added one thing to his job.' On paper it looks like he's got time. But you've got forty seconds to work with. You add one more thing and it can kill you." (Even off the reorganized Vega line, Lordstown jobs are engineered to a fraction of a second. One woman worker in the Lordstown truck plant explained to me the ways in which work is restricted by organizational "'precision": "I work with a twelve-pound air gun tightening bolts, but the guns don't always work. Sometimes I have to drop mine on the floor to make it work. Now every job has been time-studied—so having to drop the gun makes me more work.")

The Lordstown assembly line moves up and down, so that workers do not lose time on unnecessary (unproductive) stretching and bending. Chevrolet's first Lordstown coordinator boasted to *Automotive News*, when the factory opened, that "Even the conveyor system at Lordstown is unique. It has four elevations and varies in height from fourteen to seventy-two inches, according to assembly sequence, in order to bring the job closer to the operator at each station." This coordinator used almost the same words as Henry Ford, who in *My Life and Work* described his attempts at "the reduction of the necessity for thought on the part of the worker and the reduction of his movements to a minimum": "In the early part of 1914 we elevated the assembly line. We had adopted a policy of 'man-high' work; we had one line 26¼ inches and another 24½ inches from the floor." Later, in *Today and Tomorrow*, Ford explained that "stooping to the floor to pick up a tool or a part is not productive labor—therefore, all material is delivered waist-high."*

The effect of such refinements, in the 1970s as in the 1920s, is to increase the number of times each job can be performed in an hour, to increase the monotony and intensity of the job, and to increase the concentration required. Descriptions of Lordstown are thick with the sort of calculation that Henry Ford most enjoyed, as he worried over idle moments and wasted motions. If each worker took ten fewer steps each day "you will have saved 50 miles of wasted motion and misspent energy" at Highland Park each day. And Ford paid men to work, not walk. By bringing work nearer to workers, and by such advances as redesigning Vega air cleaners with 8 instead of 49 parts, GM hoped to save around $50 in labor costs on each car, or $20 million a year, or somewhere under two seconds per Vega for each Lordstown worker.

* At Lordstown, as in photographs of early Ford factories, or in Diego Rivera's Detroit murals, people work beneath an overhead conveyor belt, where the odd parts of Vegas dangle like joints of meat.

One GM executive, Joseph Godfrey, who is head of the GM Assembly Division which now manages the Lordstown Vega factories, has summarized this philosophy of modern Fordism. He complains that human productivity is hard to measure. But, he says, "If a man works sixty minutes an hour, that's full productivity. That's how I measure it." By factory organization, productivity can become "fuller" in Godfrey's sense: if each worker at Lordstown works twenty seconds more in each hour, GM will save around $1 million in a year, or 0.05 percent of its annual profit after tax. (Lordstown planning uses Fordist principles to arrange every inch of factory space, as well as every second of factory time. One woman worker at Lordstown described to me the perils of leaving work at the end of the late shift. The company had built an overpass "so we wouldn't get hit on the way to the parking lot," but the factory is surrounded by finished cars: "You're like a mouse in a puzzle looking for a way to get through, the Vegas are parked so close together.")

Automatic control and inspection, the third type of Lordstown innovation, follows from these calculations of factory rearrangement. Precision and speed of work are built into the Lordstown machinery—and the machinery is further controlled by computer processes. Such controls are an essential part of most modern auto investment, investment which, unlike the Lordstown program, does not involve expanding production, building new factories, and tearing up old equipment. Cut-price efficiency demands that employees do more work for their money: robots are expensive, but even the most stagnant auto corporation can afford the salaries of time-study engineers, and computer time for planning and rearranging. At Lordstown these techniques are used, as well as more expansionary innovations.

The Lordstown computer controllers behave like conventional, if inexorable, human supervisors. The main system is called ALPACA (Assembly Line Production and Control Activity), and "gives each operator enough [and presumably no more than enough] time to do his job." This endeavor is, again, purely Fordist. Henry Ford's biographers claim that innovations at Ford factories in the 1920s formed the basis (at least, the mechanical and conceptual rather than the electronic basis) of modern automation: Ford's cadres of foremen were certainly the inspiration for ALPACA. "Inspection," Ford wrote, "is the keynote of our production."

Another Lordstown control program, Product Assurance Control System (PACS) is intended, apparently, to help produce high-quality cars. It was described by a "product quality engineer" in the Chevrolet "quality control department" as consisting of "sixteen optical scanning devices strategically located throughout the plant." It is a "closed-loop system," and ensures that "no unresolved production problem is allowed to continue beyond a specified period." Such computer spy systems are fairly common in modern auto "quality control": much of the equipment used in the automation of production replaces inspectors and supervisors rather than unskilled workers. PACS has, however, been conspicuously unsuccessful in avoiding "unresolved production problems," and some Lordstown workers say that they have themselves seen and pointed out assembly-line defects, which are then ignored both by the computer eyes and by the human foremen. The programs in fact seem less adept at maintaining quality than at more traditional efforts—of supervision and cost control.

The sort of automated supervision attempted in the Lordstown ALPACA and PACS programs is a major objective for much of modern industry. ALPACA is only a small step towards the ideal of what one business journal describes as "the programmed responsive plant," in perfect, almost biological homeostasis, where "people would be found doing many of the things they do now, but largely under the direction of machines." In the auto industry, such a vision of automation can become grotesque. At each stage of Lordstown innovation, in mechanization, planning, and control, GM's engineers were dependent on a Fordist use of unskilled labor. Under automation of supervision, auto factory organization becomes a giant unstable hierarchy, with each level controlled by a more and more elaborate technology of reorganization, and with all controls descending to the factory floor, where unskilled workers use a fifty-year-old, nonmechanizable "knack" to assemble the parts of automobiles. As long as the auto corporations are unable to eliminate monotonous production work, they will continue to look for ever more rigorous techniques of Fordist planning, to increase the intensity and precision and predictability of work. And in the thirty-six-second jobs of Lordstown production such rigor cannot easily be found. Not only are unskilled jobs made harder with each cost saving, but the job of reorganization itself becomes harder, as inches and fractions of inches are saved in each movement, minutes and seconds and fractions of seconds in every hour.

GMAD Fordism

The last stage in GM's Lordstown reorganization was achieved with the GM Assembly Division (GMAD) takeover of plant management. The arrival of GMAD in October 1971 marked a new intensity in the disturbances that culminated in the Lordstown strike of March 1972; in the five intervening months union members registered five thousand grievances against management. GMAD's role, at Lordstown and elsewhere, was to go beyond the technological rationality of mass auto production, to a rationality of management and factory discipline. The division was founded in 1965 to control the assembly of certain GM cars, usually when more than one make was handled at a single plant.* It is now responsible for 75 percent of all GM cars in North America, for most assembly lines, and for such "rationalized" operations as coordinating the national flow of auto components. At Lordstown, as at several other plants previously operated by Chevrolet and Fisher Body, GMAD took control of joining together the final auto-assembly and auto-body-manufacturing plants; this consolidation, according to a GM executive, "rendered meaningless a significant amount of duplication of effort that existed under the previous two-management set-up. No longer was

---

* One advantage of the GMAD arrangement is that it makes GM unsuitable for simple antitrust dissolution, since the car divisions, such as Chevrolet and Buick, have few assembly facilities, and GMAD has nothing else. The division developed from the Buick-Oldsmobile assembly operation established in the 1930s, when it was decided that different cars, at different prices and with different accessories, could be assembled out of the same body components on the same production lines— as Alfred Sloan described it, "a reduction of bodies to three basic standard types."

there any need for two maintenance, two material, or two inspection departments, for example."

Beyond such acts of managerial reorganization, GMAD is charged, at Lordstown and throughout the corporation, with a more general rearrangement of factory discipline. At Lordstown this rearrangement took the form of layoffs, increased severity by foremen, the assigning of extra tasks and extra penalties for failure to perform these tasks—the sort of changes that have earned the division a national reputation for ruthless aggression. The Vega factory was designed, from the first, around an assembly-line speed of one hundred or more cars an hour, yet the new GMAD plant manager announced that "[while] there are increases in the amount of work some [workers] are doing . . . in these cases it is overdue." The manager implied that his team of production analysts had discovered tricks of cost efficiency that even the Lordstown computers had failed to imagine: "This plant, like any other new facility, was over-staffed at the start." Each of the rearrangements was designed to prevent the "waste" of time, cash, machinery, or nonproductive moments. One of the most praised mechanical innovations at Lordstown was an electrostatically controlled vat, where Vega bodies could be immersed in paint. When GMAD arrived at the factory, the new management complained that paint was being wasted, because it "would lie in crevices as the body left the vat." GMAD's complaint about Lordstown production jobs was, apparently, that expensive seconds were being wasted, in the crevices of the working day.

The GMAD intensification of discipline is a characteristic

extreme expression of modern Fordist attempts to increase auto productivity. Just as factory planning is cheaper than mechanizing jobs, and production control is cheaper than mechanical planning, so managerial discipline is cheaper than inspection or time study or other similar corporate techniques. Managers are trained to identify and eliminate waste moments. And beyond such training, the managers learn (for free) a lasting attitude of tough-mindedness, to be shared by executives and plant managers and middle managers and general supervisors and foremen on the line. (Even management toughness is based on Fordist practice. Samuel Marquis, a Ford apostate who once ran Ford's welfare department, wrote that he resigned from the company in 1921 because "the old group of executives, who at times set justice and humanity above profits and production, were gone, [and] there came to the front men whose theory was that men are more profitable to an industry when driven than led. . . . The humane treatment of employees, according to these men, would lead to the weakening of the authority of the 'boss,' and to the breaking down of discipline in the shop.")

Management tough-mindedness is itself a major issue in present automotive discontent. Workers' grievances at Lordstown concerned not only the speeding up and intensification of jobs, but also the disciplinary character of plant management—where workers must ask, and wait, to leave their jobs for one or two minutes; must ask, and wait for permission to get married on a Saturday; must show a doctor's note if they stay home when they get sick; or a note from the funeral director when they go to their father's burial; or a garage bill if they arrive at work late because their car broke down.*

This sort of discipline is not expensive for management, but it is part of the "dehumanization" of auto industry work, in which, as a Lordstown worker said to me, there is one, American, law outside the plant, and a GM law inside. A GM law which for visitors to Lordstown begins in the "employees' parking lot," where the first notice seen is in the blue and white colors of GM's corporate insignia, "This parking lot is under surveillance by closed-circuit television." A law which, at the price of a few printed signs, dominates public tours of the plant. Visitors drive through ranks of peripheral parking lots, for Vegas, trucks, executives, workers, to the employees' entrance; inside, there are more signs, and a thickening atmosphere of institutional life: straight ahead, "Don't Give Outsiders Inside Information," and, to the right of the door, a large graph of "demerits" awarded recently in the department of quality control. A Ford worker told Edmund Wilson, in 1931, that "a man checks his brains and his freedom at the door when he goes to work at Ford's." The Lordstown worker I talked to about GM's law said that America must soon move away

* The Lordstown policy on garage bills provides a striking indication of how GM watches out for its wider socioeconomic interests even while maintaining plant "authority." An officer in the local union described the procedure to me: "Everyone needs a car to get to work [the plant is completely remote from public transport, or from much housing]— but if your car breaks down you get a reprimand. If a guy is late because he had to get his car fixed, it is incumbent on him to show a receipt for repairs. Now, this might cost twenty-five dollars, and this man perhaps he's a mechanic and he could have fixed it himself for a dollar fifty."

from the "company law" to a "new law." "It's a wonder," he said, that people have not yet "tried to humanize or Americanize General Motors."

Management and supervisory toughness is built into the Lordstown factory, like the speed and accuracy of the machinery. People in the local union say that foremen are even harsher at Lordstown than in most plants: "They come here from all over GM," and "they want to get to be general foreman, up all the little steps of the ladder." "They've heard about Lordstown, and they want to say 'I make it go, I'm a part of that machine.' "* Yet the attitude of Lordstown foremen is itself part of the General Motors, GMAD machine. Supervisors rise through the corporate hierarchy, up all the little steps, by maintaining discipline, and by making "their" workers a functioning part of factory production. The Ford worker told Wilson in 1931 that "the bosses are as thick as treacle and they're always on your neck, because the man above is on their neck and Sorenson [the plant manager] is on the neck of the whole lot"; at Lordstown, as at Ford's early factories, the "rationalization" of work and authority is essential to auto production.

GMAD harshness is, in fact, an expected consequence of Fordist technology, and of Henry Ford's own attitude to human work. Automobile mass production was based on an unescapable but highly regimented use of unskilled work: it is to be expected in such an organization of production that managers and foremen should think of assembly-line work as a nearly subhuman activity, to be disciplined, circumscribed, rationalized. The week GMAD

---

* "But it's not true," one worker said, "it's the workers that make it go."

took over at Lordstown, *Automotive News* asked Mr. Godfrey, the head of the division, for his views of the "monotony of mass production": "Monotony," Godfrey answered, "is not quite the right word. There is a good deal of misunderstanding about that, but it seems to me that we have our biggest problems when we disturb that 'monotony.' The workers may complain about monotony, *but years spent in the factories leads me to believe that they like to do their jobs automatically.* If you interject new things, you spoil the rhythm of the job, and work gets fouled up." (Italics added) These opinions would have been welcomed by Henry Ford, who himself observed that "the vast majority of men want to stay put. They want to be led. They want to have everything done for them and to have no responsibility"—who wrote "some of our tasks are extremely monotonous . . . but then, also many minds are very monotonous." Godfrey has summarized most lucidly the spirit of GMAD, and of modern Fordism: the implicit hope that production work can be reduced to a disciplined part of a great machine, to work for human automata.

"Treat Me with Respect and I will give you Top Quality Work with Less Effort."

People at Lordstown find the same conditions of work that Ford workers found in the 1920s and 1930s: the same precise restriction of jobs, as they try to make time to drop their faulty air guns; similar disciplinary attitudes, with notes from the funeral director, and permission to leave the line, and foremen on the necks of other foremen; the same "un-American" laws inside the employees' factory entrance. More than most other industries, the auto business sustains an old pattern of production, where unskilled work is both essential and degraded, and where people literally and metaphorically serve machines. For a group of women workers I talked to at Lordstown, it was exactly this situation, with people less important than machines, that summarized the conditions of Lordstown work: where management offices were air-conditioned, while people worked with machines in extremes of heat and cold, where "GM is the richest company in the world and our roof leaks when it rains," and where "the other day an [electrical] transformer blew up just where I work; we thought the plant had been bombed, and we sat there waiting in the dark for an hour and a half while they tried to get in touch with Detroit to close the plant down." Where the factory nurses say, "You didn't do that to yourself in the plant," so we can't treat it, and the doctors are like "veterinarians," and where "we matter less to them than machines or tools." Where, as one of the women described it, "Some of the machines have written on them 'Treat Me with Respect and I will give you Top Quality Work with Less Effort,' and the GM sign. I said we should have that printed on sweatshirts, and wear them to work . . . but we wouldn't be able to keep them on for five minutes, we'd be sent home for disrespect. We should have a whole lot made, and all wear them together. . . . They couldn't send the whole shop home."

5
Modern Times

GM provided an official explanation for the Lordstown disturbances some six months after the 1972 strike. The occasion of this explanation was a speech given by GM's vice-president for labor relations—to the Rotary Club in Flint, Michigan (an area where GM employs more than a third of all workers, and where the founders of GM first established, in the 1900s, what Alfred Sloan described as a "small society of auto and parts manufacturers"). The GM vice-president, George Morris, assumed that his audience had heard about "such things as blue collar blues, assembly line boredom, the new work force, and worker alienation": "Unfortunately," he said, "I think we have just begun to hear complaints about how awful it is to work in the auto industry."

The stated purpose of the Flint speech was to "set the record straight," and show that "an auto industry job, like that in any industry, can be as rewarding as a person is willing to make it." To this end, Mr. Morris determined to provide the "facts" of the Lordstown strike, "where much of the controversy over jobs in our industry originated." According to Morris's facts, the Lordstown strike followed from the consolidation of Lordstown operations, under the GM Assembly Division, and more specifically from three main issues: "manpower reduction," "disciplinary actions," and "the negotiation of new local agreements." Each of these three issues, Morris said, was "expected," "typical," and "old hat."* Asking, rhetorically, if there was anything "really novel" about the Lordstown situation, Morris observed that strikes over working conditions were a normal consequence of corporate reorganization, and were not "really related" to "boredom on the assembly line" or "the age of the workers." In 1968–69 GMAD had consolidated and reorganized its Chevrolet and Fisher Body operations at six plants: "Note the fact that strikes occurred following each of these consolidations. I'm not boasting, I'm just relating relevant history." The division later took over four more plants, including Lordstown, and "Thus, ten consolidations have produced eight strikes. It should be apparent,

---

* "As might be expected, the manpower reductions which were effectuated [in late 1971] by the new GMAD management were strongly resisted by employees and the local union. This resistance typically took the form of a slow-down by employees, refusals to follow instructions, other acts of insubordination, and even a number of instances of sabotage. Management invoked disciplinary action against many employees for this kind of misconduct. This also was typical. Disciplinary action along with manpower reductions thus became an issue in the strike. Again—typical. So two of the three main issues in the strike were old hat. The third main issue was even more so [and] concerned the negotiation of new local agreements."

to employ an understatement, that these consolidations are difficult to accomplish without conflict."

For GM, workers' discontent as expressed at Lordstown was an unexceptionable consequence, if not of auto industry work, at least of the improvements in organizational efficiency to which modern auto corporations aspire. Mr. Morris was talking about those Lordstown rearrangements associated specifically with GMAD—but the corporation's innovations in mechanical technology, as seen earlier, tended to have much the same purpose and effect on work as its managerial advances. Even at the Lordstown factories, which used more new capital investment, of a more ambitious sort, than most auto projects, GMAD's efforts amounted to a refinement of existing factory organization. GM's descriptions of "typical" factory life, with "refusals to follow instructions," "acts of insubordination," "misconduct," and "disciplinary action," could summarize the authoritarian management attitudes, the attempt to treat people as small parts of machine production, which for many workers was a major issue of Lordstown working relations, more important even than the repetitiveness of assembly jobs.

The "Flint version" of the Lordstown strike raises questions about the implications of Lordstown production for the auto industry beyond GM or GMAD. In arguing that strikes and "insubordination" are inevitable, Mr. Morris admitted a dramatically dismal view of automotive labor relations; "conflict," from this GM perspective, was a fact of business life. In emphasizing specific rearrangements of Lordstown production, Morris then showed, not so much that "assembly line boredom" is unimportant, as that issues to do with the character of work are implicit in even the most "old hat" of production issues. Until 1972, the new Lordstown factories were acclaimed as models of advanced or Utopian auto technology. If, as Morris seems to imply, subsequent Lordstown unrest was also "typical" of auto production, the automotive future looks worse than troubled.

GM's Flint perspective can provide some introduction to this future. The typicality of Lordstown, and of Lordstown Fordism, will become clear from the general situation of auto labor relations, from factory conditions outside the assembly phase of auto production, and from the common characteristics of automotive work. It will be clear, for example, that for some modern management experts on "blue collar" unrest, Lordstown work is representative of most auto production jobs. If Lordstown does then appear as typical, it will be possible to ask whether Fordist principles are *technologically* necessary for auto production; whether in production, as in selling, the auto industry is fixed on its past successes, as management inertia, bad working conditions, and Fordist mass-production technology together assume the character of an irresistible auto imperative; and whether, in conclusion, the possibilities remain encouraging for changing auto technology, or for improving automotive work.

Labor Relations

Mr. Morris's observation—"not boasting"—about the prevalence of auto strikes applies beyond Lordstown and GMAD's eight troubled plants. The auto industry, now as in the past, leads U.S. industry in most indicators of industrial unrest. Truculent corporate spokesmen complain about the general prevalence of strikes outside the pattern of national collective bargaining: GM is not the only corporation affected, nor assembly plants the only factories. Auto workers are famously likely to stay home from work: Ford Motor Company claimed in 1970 that absenteeism had "doubled" or "tripled" in ten years, while such average figures "mask[ed] the crippling effects often felt on a key production operation or line." The auto "quit rate" is similarly famous: one recent study of factory work found that more than half of all new unskilled auto workers, in the "major northern production centers," leave their jobs within the first year at work. (Throughout the auto industry, visitors hear stories about workers who decide to quit. Lordstown workers tell how "four men from a steel mill," in the depressed local steel industry, came to work in the new truck-plant paint shop, "and they lasted till lunchtime." When I first went to Lordstown, in 1970, a union officer told me that after the Chevrolet plant first started operating, years before the advent of GMAD or the Vega, new workers were "coming in and quitting" so fast that the local union could not "even keep our files up to date": "Young kids, straight out of high school, who didn't know what working was like. They just couldn't take the pace, and they quit.")

Such manifestations of auto industry unrest have been well known since the earliest days of the international auto business. The present American experience is not exceptional: absenteeism was about as high at Ford factories before 1914 as it is today, while absenteeism and labor turnover in, for example, the Swedish auto industry was until recently almost twice as high as in the U.S. industry.

A particularly vivid account of contemporary American labor/management relations was given in a GM "position paper" produced during the 1970 contract negotiations between the companies and the UAW—negotiations in which GM led national management resistance to union demands. According to the paper, discipline had broken down in auto factories, and plant managers observed an alarming increase in "tardiness, loitering, failure to follow instructions, and abuse of employee facilities." Production schedules were "disrupted repeatedly by 'crisis' situations and strikes," while "careless workmanship . . . appear[ed] to be increasing."

The most bitter section of the position paper demanded a revision of the GM sickness and accident benefit program —and provided a bleak view of workers' "job satisfaction." Illness and recovery provisions had "deteriorated badly," according to the paper, and were too generous, notably where "vague" or "subjective" diseases were involved. Workers were staying off the job because of accidents. They took too long to recover. More and more workers were reporting "strains and sprains and nervous diseases," subjective illnesses which were hard to diagnose. All this nervousness was costing the corporation a lot of money. The sickness benefits "promote[d] a sense of security and, for some employees, a desire to stay on sick leave."

Automotive Phases

Auto assembly work has been since the 1910s famously unpleasant and unpopular—for reasons which, as at Lordstown, have to do with the foundations of Fordist technology. Yet auto work now seems unsatisfactory not only for its mechanical routines. The conditions of Lordstown work— measured, repetitive, unskilled—exist throughout the auto industry, in a more or less developed form. Many of the techniques and management attitudes of auto assembling are found in auto-parts factories. Components factories, where 60 percent of all auto workers are employed, reflect some of the major achievements of Henry Ford's standard- ized mass-production technology; Chaplin based *Modern Times* on the horrors of Detroit factories, yet the machinery in the film seems to fit parts production rather than auto assembly. At each stage of auto production, from final as- sembly and body assembly back through stamping and small-parts manufacturing to engine production, similar methods apply. One industrial sociologist even argues that "all other operations in the [auto] industry" are coordi- nated to the needs of final assembly: "Because the line sets the rhythm of production in the industry, most off-line jobs, particularly in assembly plants, take on many of the charac- teristics of assembly line work." In their intensification of work, GM's Lordstown engineers were improving upon organizational methods found in parts as well as assembly plants, now as in the past.

Stamping operations, one phase back in auto production from the assembly line, are less famously nasty than as- sembly operations. Yet stamping factories—about one in four of all auto workers work in stamping and small-parts plants—sustain the pace of final production: the new Lordstown stamping plant, for example, was built for Vega production, and steel moves on an overhead conveyor belt

from stamping to body to final assembly. Some engineers
outside the auto industry argue that the often unskilled and
nonautomated (and appallingly noisy) stamping process is,
if anything, more unpleasant than assembly-line production.
Frederick W. Taylor first developed his techniques of scientific management and of time-and-motion study at metal
stamping plants of the 1890s; a modern British technologist
has said of the parts-stamping operations at Ford's River
Rouge factory that "the men who feed and unload the
presses are in effect chained to their machines, forced to
perform to the machine rhythm—endlessly the same monotonous task—with no sense of identity with the end product, or opportunity to contribute to product quality or
production efficiency. This arrangement serves neither man
nor machine well." In such factories, at least, conditions are
close to the Lordstown model.

Of all auto operations those in engine factories and
foundries have moved furthest from Fordist practice, and
from the Lordstown ways of organizing unskilled work.
The factories which produce Vega engines, for example, are
highly automated (and hundreds of miles around Lake Erie
from Lordstown); at Ford, the British technologist found
that engine and transmission components were produced
"in a totally different ambience" from assembly or parts-
stamping operations, with comparatively little unskilled,
repetitive work. But the engine plants must still produce
their parts for final assembly, and foundry work is also the
most dangerous of all auto operations. Like other compo-
nent plants, engine factories remain subject to the rigorous
criteria of cost efficiency and machine supremacy which
shape most automotive production—a supremacy that is

perhaps particularly overpowering in expensive, empty engine factories.

Through all these operations and auto phases, time control remains the basis of auto technology. As at Lordstown, jobs are subdivided to serve the rhythms of mechanical production. A recent study of work in eleven major American industries, the Shelley Report on job improvement, devoted a long and pessimistic section to the automobile industry. (The study was written for the American Foundation on Automation and Employment, and financed by the Ford Foundation. It set out to "beseech business to deflect some of its productive energy toward general enrichment programs for employees in order somehow to counteract the [present] dissatisfaction with institutions . . . which is predicted to spread to the industrial situation.") The report found that the automobile industry as a whole "lends itself to measurement of a man's work like few other industries": "More than 70 percent of the work force has its moves detailed down to the second, operates in set work stations, and performs generally short-cycle repetitive tasks." Time-and-motion studies were found to be the "fulcrum" of production, and a most "volatile" factor in labor relations —in the 1970s as in the 1920s, or as they were when J. Z. DeLorean, GM's leading apostle of Lordstown efficiency, started his auto career as a time-and-motion man in a Chrysler body plant: DeLorean reminisced recently to a reporter, saying, "I decided I was going to be an industrial engineer, which at the time was sort of fashionable . . . [but] you'd go in there and, boy, all those big guys'd do everything but throw spare parts at you! They'd hoot and scream, and I decided, jeez, I really don't want to do this."

Work

When Henry Ford introduced the Five-Dollar Day in 1914, he boasted that Ford workers used a minimum of skills or talents; and auto skills, as at Lordstown, have been reduced continuously ever since. In auto assembling, according to the Shelley Report, 80 percent of employees "work on the line and are considered unskilled"; in machining and engine-foundry operations most workers are semiskilled, while in stamping and small-parts factories 65 percent of all employees are unskilled or "entry level." One union official told me that he had found throughout the industry a "continuation of delimiting the worker's role." In assembly plants, he said, the only work with any "creativity" was in the tiny minority of jobs for "electricians or maintenance pipe fitters." Beyond the specific boredom and monotony of automotive jobs, there remains a degradation of work implicit in the Fordist reduction of tasks, in factory discipline and management attitudes, in the inevitability of machine processes.

The modern auto business comes close to realizing Frederick Taylor's ambition, of "gathering in on the part of those on the management's side all the great mass of traditional knowledge which in the past has been in the heads of the workmen and in the physical knack and skill of the workman." It employs a higher proportion of unskilled workers than most other major U.S. industries. Training for unskilled workers is usually minimal, a matter of a few hours. The Shelley Report found that "entry into the [auto] industry is now virtually without significant criteria—physical ability and desire to work being the prime consideration"—

the same consideration that was described by an early Ford worker in Céline's *Journey to the End of the Night*: "What he liked about Ford's, the old Russian explained confidentially, was that they would hire anyone and anything."

A new auto worker has less chance than workers in most jobs of acquiring new skills, or of moving to another job in the factory, or of receiving on-the-job training. The Shelley Report wrote that of all the industries it studied, the two with "the least opportunities for the bulk of entry level workers" were the motor-vehicle and apparel businesses. Working conditions in the apparel industry have been famously brutal at least since 1864, when the British government Children's Employment Commission investigated the industrial sewing machine: Marx's observations of nineteenth-century factory rationalization, of the tendency in "automatic" factories "to equalize and reduce to one and the same level every kind of work that has to be done by the minders of the machines," were based on the British textile and apparel industries. The Shelley Report found in the modern motor-vehicle industry a particularly high proportion of "dead end jobs," which "do not provide a reasonable expectation of advancement"; it observed that "the only meaningful upgrade is really out of progression, and involves moving to the apprentice program or to supervision," and that such progression as there is should be regarded "more in terms of a reward for longevity than a true upgrade."

The restriction of automotive work is measured by the fact that almost all auto workers make the same amount of money: the auto industry has the lowest spread of production wage rates of any industry studied by the U.S. government. In industries, such as petroleum refining, where goods are produced continuously rather than by assembly and parts manufacturing, workers supervise complex and expensive capital equipment (as they do in some auto engine operations) ; in the steel industry, which has changed its technology much more than the auto business, the Shelley Report found "thirty-three different rates of pay, each . . . determined through an elaborate weighing of task requirements." These comparisons do not imply that jobs in the steel or the (often noxious) petrochemical industry are pleasant, but they indicate, at least, the peculiarly depressed status of work in auto production.

The devaluation of work, where, as at Lordstown, workers "matter less than machines or tools," is found throughout the auto industry. According to the Shelley Report, the motor-vehicle and apparel industries are "mass producers with tasks simplified to the point that almost anyone, once trained, can perform the tasks of other employees throughout the facility"; the auto industry, more than almost any other business, uses its many unskilled workers as interchangeable parts of machine production. Corporations schedule arduous and unpredictable working hours. Overtime is compulsory, and this compulsion is a major issue in contract bargaining: a letter published with the 1970 contract between the United Auto Workers and GM provides that workers may, in specified circumstances, refuse overtime after working for thirteen consecutive days. The relative importance of work and machine time was shown clearly by the Ford Motor Company in a lavish book, *Ford at Fifty*, published for the company's anniversary in 1953. A centerfold explains "How a Car Is Assembled"; seventy-three drawings show a car moving through an assembly plant, from "Floorpan," at "9 Hours 24 Minutes," to "Test Drive," at "0 Hours 0 Minutes." The signs proclaiming assembly time are large and bold and dominate the picture. At each stage of production, tiny workers are dwarfed by the line and the oversized Ford cars—as they add, for example, "Deck Lid Weatherstrip," at "4 Hours 52 Minutes."

Henry Ford used time-study engineers to investigate the movements which constitute a job; in GMAD's operations, computer supervisors calculate the lowest common or possible characteristics of work. The *Wall Street Journal* describes "GMAD's use of its relatively new system of computerized time studies": "GM feeds time-study data from all of its plants into a computer. The computer then catalogs the readings, breaks every possible job down into elements of work, and then comes up with an average time allotment based on the inputs."

Work in auto production is reduced to "manhours," or "manminutes," or simply to dollars. Auto managers talk about manhours in units of thousands or tens of thousands. When I visited GM headquarters in Detroit (of which occasion more later), one of the executives I spoke with described a company training project, which eventually paid off in "hard factors" of efficiency: the plant manager had meanwhile spent "25,000 hours on training," and, "Miss Rothschild, that has a hell of a price tag on it." The Shelley Report found similar attitudes when it asked auto executives about the possibility of increasing training and orientation time for new workers, in an attempt to reduce discontent: "One official [in an unnamed auto corporation] indicated the cost to the company to give a new man one hour more of nonproductive company time—not to mention a full day or a week—would be astronomical and practically prohibitive to such a cost-conscious industry." (These remarks reflect the management attitudes about which Lordstown workers complained. One local union officer, who said of company representatives that "we are about as important to them as a chair or an ashtray," told me he had a recurrent fear, during negotiations with GM, that "if they had a strong desire they could just evacuate the buildings and leave." The idea of GM abandoning a troublesome plant, or troublesome workers, may seem odd; but Mr. Godfrey of GMAD has exactly expressed, in a published interview, this interchangeability of workers and work forces. He argued that most auto workers "know what they were getting into": "They complain and yet, if we closed Lordstown down and then reopened, we'd get 50,000 applications"—for these depressed but well-paid jobs.)

The lack of skills, and opportunity, and valued work, together represent the conditions of auto manufacturing—where an early-twentieth-century technology and early-twentieth-century management attitudes, at Lordstown and throughout the industry, have shaped work into a depressed commodity. A bleakly clear picture of these conditions was given in a recent national survey of worker attitudes, sponsored by the Department of Labor. Part of the survey measured "workers' overall levels of satisfaction with their jobs," and it included a calculation of the "characteristics of workers or their jobs most highly correlated with overall job satisfaction." Of the nineteen characteristics mentioned, few had to do with pay, or with demographic factors such as age. The seven characteristics most highly correlated with job satisfaction all concerned working conditions—and all are conspicuously lacking in the auto industry. They could together provide a checklist of what automotive work is not. *One, "Having a 'nurturant' supervisor (e.g., one who takes a personal interest in those he supervises and goes out of his way to praise good work)"*: the nonnurturant nature of auto foremen is famous, and sometimes, as at Lordstown, seems inherent in Fordist technology. *Two, "Receiving adequate help, assistance, authority, time, information, machinery, tools, and equipment to do the job"*: authority and information have little to do with most auto jobs, and machines are often supplied with workers, rather than the other way around. *Three, "Feeling that one's employer handles promotions fairly"*: hardly applies to the auto industry, given the general lack of promotion opportunities. *Four, "Having a supervisor who does not supervise too closely"*: intense supervision, by human and automatic supervisors and as determined by machine processes, is essential to present auto production. *Five, "Having a technically competent supervisor"*: in assembly plants, at least, even supervisors have little opportunity to learn skills and competence. *Six, "Having autonomy in matters that affect one's work"*: this characteristic would contradict the entire development of auto production. *Seven, "Having a job with 'enriching' demands (e.g., a job that demands that one learn new things, have a high level of skill, be creative, and do a variety of different things)"*: this characteristic is derisory in the context of automotive work.

The conditions of automotive production, based on an old and restrictive use of work, have the same relation to early mass production as modern auto marketing has to the sales methods of the 1930s and 1950s. In each situation, automotive management obeys past industrial forces, which assume the power of irresistible necessity. These forces, in the case of auto production, appear as mysterious or scientific, determined by the objective technology of automobiles, of stamped-out metal parts assembled into cars. To many corporate executives, as will be clear later, Fordist production is a fact of business life; these managers cannot understand that there should be any contradiction between human aspirations and the organization of work that seems implicit in Fordist technology.

The extent of management fears about attempting changes in auto working conditions will become evident from corporate pronouncements: there are also "objective" reasons for this inertia, and for the apparent inevitability of Fordist engineering, as found at Lordstown and throughout the industry. Automobiles are produced according to an old technology, a technology that shapes work and the design of automobiles. Technology need not be mysterious or mystifying: when mass production was new and exciting Henry Ford described his factories down to the smallest ball bearing, and modern, science-based industries are eager to display their own new and exciting technologies (the recent "spectacular advances on the [American] technical front" that for *Business Week* included "the electronic computer, numerically controlled machine tools, lasers, integrated circuits, and a raft of exotic plastics than can perform almost any job"). The main difficulty in finding out about

present auto engineering is that the modern auto corporations, except at Lordstown and a few new engine plants,
are not particularly proud of their technological achievements. But there is enough information about auto conditions—from, for example, business surveys of national
productivity, or from studies of technology and work enrichment—to provide at least some idea of the technological
base of modern auto production.

The original achievements of Fordist technology consisted of replacing skilled work with machine production,
in assembly and parts manufacturing, and of organizing
rationally the complex collections of parts that were to be
made into automobiles. The industrial attraction and romance of Detroit reflected these two achievements: on the
one hand, the power and the wheels within wheels of the
American machine age; on the other, the almost unimaginable size of auto corporations, where steel from Iron
Mountain, and miles of glass from Minnesota, and tools
engineered to a ten-thousandth of an inch on the Johanssen
scale, and tires made of Brazilian rubber, and hundreds of
millions of metal bolts all arrived at River Rouge, all at the
instant when Henry Ford needed them.

This second, logistical, achievement is still the proudest
part of auto production.* General Motors is still the largest
industrial corporation in history, and its auto components

* Ford's fiftieth-anniversary book boasted that the River Rouge plant
"could supply all the homes in Boston with electric power. It uses
as much water as Detroit, Washington, and Cincinnati combined. It has
110 miles of railroad tracks and 22 Diesel locomotives, 81 miles of
conveyors and four bus lines." More modestly, it also notes that "visitors
who see hundreds of cars being assembled together wonder why blue
wheels somehow never seem to arrive here with a green body. . . ."

still flow punctually across America and the world. At Lordstown, the Vega plant is piled with crates of auto components, each marked as urgent, with the name and address of the supplying firm. Thousands of screws and tires line the aisles, with paint from Du Pont and engines from Chevrolet at Tonawanda, New York, and a railroad freight car at one end of the assembly building called the "Main-Line of Mid-America." But the other achievement of early Fordism, in mechanical production, now seems to belong to an old technology, surpassed in science and industrial attraction. It is exactly, in fact, its continued dependence on a once magnificent mechanical technology that has caused the present depression of auto engineering.

The auto industry, at each phase of production, is dominated by its millions of metal and mechanical components. Work, as seen above, is often similar in assembly and in parts production, and both operations use a similarly early technology. Alfred Sloan began his account of GM's technical achievements with the statement that "General Motors is an engineering organization. Our operation is to cut metal and in so doing to add value to it": as an industry based on metal cutting, the auto business is fixed to a technology of the early decades of the century, of the American metal age. Henry Ford's innovations in the standardization of parts production (as distinct from his assembly-line achievements) were derived from the nineteenth-century manufacture of metal mass-production goods, rifles, Colt revolvers, typewriters, sewing machines: Ford cars, like these products, were made out of more or less simple metal parts.

These origins of auto production are shown clearly in

the industrial history of Detroit. Detroit was able to support the new automobile industry not only because it was near the coal of Pennsylvania and the iron ore of Minnesota, but also because it had been in the nineteenth century an industrial city, a center for stoves, adding machines, freight cars, metal beds. The technology of early-twentieth-century Modern Times was expressed most clearly in the cutting and stamping of metal parts, to be made into revolvers or adding machines or automobiles—the sort of commodities for which Frederick Taylor designed his scientific management of production, achieving, as John Dos Passos wrote of Taylor in *U.S.A.*, "more steel rails more bicycles more spools of thread more armorplate for battleships more bedpans more barbedwire more needles more lightningrods more ballbearings more dollarbills."

Assembly technology is, as much as or more than parts manufacturing, a development of early-twentieth-century mechanical production. Beyond its dependence on standardized metal parts, the auto industry requires a conveyor-belt technique of final assembly. Automobiles use not only stamped parts but also more complex engine, and electrical, and, recently, electronic components—yet the ways of assembling thousands of parts on a moving line remain similar, whether the parts are simple, or metal, or electronic. Like parts production, auto assembling developed Taylorist ideas about the use of labor. The anniversary volume, *Ford at Fifty,* comments cautiously that "some people say Henry Ford got the idea for his moving assembly line from watching men in the Chicago stockyards cut meat as it was passed by them on overhead conveyors": assembly technology, as at Lordstown, depends upon manual work, cutting meat or fixing wheels, and at its simplest it is a way of allowing workers to assemble things faster and more "easily" than they would without a moving line.

In the industrial imagination of the early twentieth century, these developments represented an amazing expansion of the strength and productivity of work, as American auto factories became the monuments of world mechanization: Henry Ford's biographers write that Soviet workers in the 1920s "emblazoned" the name of Ford on banners, as "emblematic of a new era." Yet by the 1950s and 1960s the U.S. auto industry and other metal-based or assembly industries had lost their early technological romance. The monumental American industries were now the ones that made chemicals, or "exotic" plastics, or computers, or electronic weapons, commodities that required minimal unskilled work. If automotive technology now seemed anachronistic, it was exactly because of its continuing dependence on manual work, however strong and productive. The prospect of regulating more and more precisely hundreds of thousands of unskilled jobs becomes increasingly dismal, even with the advanced techniques of supervision used at Lordstown. (Many of the auto industry's troubles were shared with metal-products businesses, now among the most depressed and unadventurous of all U.S. industries, and with other assembly industries.* American appliance and con-

---

* Warren, Ohio, the town nearest to Lordstown, was by coincidence a pure example of a metal-cutting city fallen on bleak days, at least until the expansion of GM's new factories. The local Chamber of Commerce distributes a handbook called "Warren—A Place, a People, a Way of Life"; Warren has had one of the highest rates of unemployment in Ohio, but for "Warren—A Place" the city was "ideally located in the heart of the great Mahoning Valley steel district." It specialized in a finely Taylorist collection of products: "steel doors, electric motors, dies and molds, compasses, drinking fountains, aluminum extrusions, transformers, car bumpers, butted steel tubing, cold-rolled sheets. . . ."

sumer-goods industries, which use manual assembly techniques, are also depressed, and troubled by foreign
competition. For these industries, unskilled work is a regrettable necessity, to be found, whenever possible, in the
television factories of Taiwan, or among the "nimble-
fingered" women who assemble electronic components in
South Korea.)

Modern "monumental" industries enjoy the simultaneous
successes that the auto industry experienced in the 1920s.
They benefit from "spectacular advances on the technical
front"; they grow fast; they use large amounts of capital for
every production worker that they employ. Some of these
industries, such as the computer and advanced aerospace
businesses, are based on scientific knowledge, and are
hardly comparable to mass-manufacturing industries in that
they employ a large proportion of technically qualified
workers. Other advanced modern industries, including the
continuous-process petroleum and electricity businesses, are
themselves mass manufacturers, and as such present a
dramatic contrast to the automobile and other metal-based
or assembly industries—using considerably more capital for
every worker than the automobile industry, and a relatively
high proportion of skilled to unskilled and of nonproduction
(including scientific and technical) to production workers.
Industries based on petroleum, on some chemicals, and on
energy have been among the most expansionary businesses
of postwar America: fertilizers, detergents, synthetic or-
ganic chemicals led much of the growth of the manufacturing economy. Plastics, such as *Business Week*'s "raft of
exotic plastics than can perform almost any job," now seem
among the most "modern" of all commodities, as metal

products and automobiles were in the 1920s: IBM boasts
that it has developed a "superplastic" metal, a zinc-
aluminum alloy that "can be formed like plastic." For the
postwar continuous-process industries, as for the auto business in the 1920s, products and production and a use of
work have together created a situation of manufacturing
modernity, of expansionary technological advance.

The contrasts between (older) automotive and (newer)
continuous-process production have been described in rapt
detail by business engineers, including those engineers who
now criticize automotive technology from the perspective of
work organization. D. T. N. Williamson, the British scien-
tist who described the stamping plant at Ford's Rouge
factory, attacked automotive processes on the grounds of
failings in efficiency and modernity, and also because present management trends, in the automotive and similar
industries, are "steadily veering into opposition with the
values, aspirations, and expectations of the people who
have to keep the industrial system going."*

The unsatisfactory character of most auto manufacturing
is, according to Williamson, "the result of continual striving
to produce at improved cost efficiency in an insulated company environment employing a state-of-the-art technology.
At the time each method (of production, in auto and other
assembly industries) was introduced, it was judged to be
the most effective, but both the criteria of judgement and
technology have changed in the interim, so that what was
once conventional wisdom is now anachronistic and inap-

---

* Williamson, an engineer with a British capital-equipment firm, was
addressing the British Royal Society on the subject of the "Anachronistic
Factory."

propriate in terms not only of efficiency but also of human values." This anachronistic character of auto production is presented as being in dramatic contrast with continuous-flow processes. Williamson compares the efficiency of flow-line and process industries, as measured in output and capital per worker: his argument reflects the industrial romance of the "plastic age." Process plants benefit from the development "after the Second World War, of control theory and electrical analog and digital computers," and "this area has managed to attract the best brains in chemical and control engineering. . . . In a modern oil refinery, chemical works, or power station, a few men control and maintain plant which generates physical wealth at an unprecedented rate": Williamson concludes that "the current technology in the process industries represents the summit of man's achievement in manufacturing."

Automobile production is thus presented as "anachronistic" not only in its use of work (and, indirectly, in its contribution to the "inexorable rise of industrial unrest") but also in terms of managerial and technological efficiency. Williamson ends his paper by quoting approvingly from an article, called "The Anachronistic Factory," by a Harvard professor of business administration. This professor is much less ready than Williamson to attack specific industries, whether in metal-goods production or in final assembly, but he pronounces that "cost" should no longer be the main criterion in factory design, and that Taylorist ideas of work measurement are no longer effective. His argument, given that work measurement and an obsession with costs are among the most famous characteristics of auto production, reflects the modern management view of auto technology that Williamson presented. "How ironic," the professor writes, "that in production, where scientific management techniques began, these conventional approaches now seem out of date and out of tune with the social and economic facts of the times. Production management is perhaps bringing to an end a long cycle that began with innovation and new concepts for accomplishing productivity, developed in maturity of ideas, subsequently grew into a 'conventional wisdom,' and finally arrived at the point where we now see obsolescence."

The technological decline of the auto industry affects all the interrelated troubles of modern auto maturity. The mass production of complex cars fits on the one hand a Fordist organization of work, and on the other hand the Sloanist arrangements for elaborate selling. A rigorous regulation of production, as found at Lordstown and throughout the industry, is inherent in the development of auto technology, and in the shape of automobiles as assemblages of metal and other parts. In the stamping and cutting of standardized parts, workers actually operate and feed the machines that cut metal; in auto assembling, workers actually put parts together, with their tasks regulated according to scientific principles of management. So long as automobiles are complex collections of parts, they seem to demand a labor-based assembly technique—as one GM executive (Thomas Fitzgerald, of whom more later) has written, "A narrow use of labor," with "stopwatch measurement," is intrinsic to "rationalized work systems" based on industrial engineering, while machine control of work was "made necessary" by "the utilities of standardization and of interchangeability of parts."

Upgraded auto selling requires the manufacture of elaborate cars, as more options and improvements are added to basic auto bodies—year after year, in the development of Sloanist variety, and minute after minute, as cars move down assembly lines. Since the 1920s and 1930s, auto marketing has demanded the sort of complexity in auto design that limits the possibility of automating auto assembling: in Alfred Sloan's words, quoted earlier, "The production engineer's problems in creating techniques for mass production often [in the early 1920s] caused him to want to hold up design changes in the product. They were headaches to him. But by the mid-twenties, the product engineer had begun to feel the influence of the sales people. He then began to yield to market considerations." The effect of these market and styling considerations, which became dominant by the early 1930s, has been summarized by Joseph Godfrey of the GM Assembly Division: "If we made the same car today that we did in 1933 we probably could do it quicker. But cars today are different. They have much more equipment on them."

Technological inertia creates automotive troubles, as work organization suits auto production, which in turn suits automobile design. This "suitability" of technique is found generally in the booms of rising industries, and in the declines of depressed industries. Automotive innovation was most successful in the 1920s, when auto sales expanded fast, and when the auto corporations invested lavishly in capital and research: expansionary modern industries, with rapidly growing sales, experience a similar suitability of technical advance, where new automated technologies, producing new products, require a new arrangement of work.

In recent auto difficulties, all the weight of economic immobility reinforces the depression of auto technology, as
auto corporations hesitate to build new factories, or to
abandon old machines, or to hire new scientists.

Certain advances in automated production cannot be
used in (are not "suitable" for) auto manufacturing: cars
and their parts are not, for example, the kinds of commodities that can move continuously and automatically through
a factory—unlike plastics, or petroleum, or even soft drinks
and matches, car parts cannot be made to flow continuously
along pipelines. But other innovations, while technically
applicable to auto production, are ignored, because of the
auto corporations' economic and strategic inertia. At Lordstown, as *Fortune* revealed, workers hand materials to the
Unimate robots because their simple handling jobs were
"too expensive" to automate; Williamson writes that automatic assembly methods in the auto and other assembly
industries, "when technically ready for introduction . . . are
unlikely to be cheaper than the corresponding manual methods. An example can be cited of a well-known instrument
manufacturing company which redesigned a clock to be
assembled automatically. Although the automatic assembly
machines were very simple, they were never made, because
it was found that the assembly procedure had been so simplified that girls could now do it more cheaply than the
automatic machines." For the automobile industry, such
calculations are usually of critical importance. Alfred Sloan
quotes a speech by a GM technologist which expresses
clearly the automotive relationship between economics and
technological change. This GM executive, discussing "mis-
conceptions" about "automation," pronounces that "The

decision to mechanize or not to mechanize a production process or operation involves much more than the number of repetitive operations; it involves a good many fundamentals of economics. . . . By economic solution we mean the solution to the problem which will provide the best return on our capital investment."

The forces that affect corporate technological inertia are shown most clearly in the troubled possibilities for auto change. Any radical change in auto production would require correspondingly great changes of auto design and marketing, of basic automotive strategy. The likely consequences of such change can be illustrated in the case of simple, urban cars, designed not for long-distance high-speed highway travel, but to cover short distances in crowded cities. Such simple cars, with few parts, could be produced cheaply, by highly automated procedures which use comparatively little unskilled and circumscribed work. GM aspired to these benefits but fell short of them when it designed Vegas and the Lordstown processes for fast and easy assembly: a GM "project manager" told *Automotive News* that "Our challenge was to design for simplicity"; Vega sedan bodies had 578 parts made out of 1,231 different pieces, while the bodies of full-size Chevrolet Impalas had 996 parts, made out of 3,500 pieces.

Still further simplification of auto design would allow auto manufacturers to use new production techniques, for automatic assembly and also for parts production. Vegas are made with some molded plastic parts: even simpler cars could be built out of a few large plastic or fiberglass components which could be manufactured more or less continuously. Such cars could be produced very soon. A representative of the Owens-Corning Fiberglas corporation has suggested that fiberglass "city cars," roughly the size of present small Hondas, could be on sale within five years. These cars could be assembled from two or three basic body components: as the representative puts it, "With a car that small, it is essential to get the labor out of it." (A recent advertisement by Owens-Corning explains further some of the hopes and perils of automotive simplification. Two cars are displayed, with their disassembled front ends; one car is described as "The Old Way," "Design, Manufacture, and Assemble 10 metal parts to make one auto front end," and the other as "The Fiberglas Way," "Mold the identical front end in Fiberglas-Reinforced Plastic. Only one lightweight part. Speeds assembly, saves money. . . ." The auto corporations will be able to simplify their front ends—but beyond the ten metal parts there are, for Vegas or Impalas, thousands more parts, not all of which can be molded in the Reinforced Plastic Way.)

The production of simple city cars could transform auto technology, and improve auto work—but it would at the same time deny the entire history of American marketing elaboration, from Alfred Sloan's youth to the recent up-grading of the Vega. For the last forty years, almost all alterations in auto design have emphasized "improvements" in the appearance and appurtenances of cars, in-creasing the number of parts to be added on, while the basic automobile remains unchanged. The development of the Vega reveals this contradiction between auto marketing and productive improvement. Even GM's simplest cars, Vegas, are still sold according to the most traditional principles of variety marketing, with the most conventional complement of options. They look like hundreds of older American and foreign auto models. Their production at Lordstown does not approach the ideal of advanced and automated assembling. Their 578 body parts—418 less than in an Impala—are still far from the simplicity of city cars whose bodies can be molded out of three fiberglass components.

Auto ventures in selling tiny and basic city cars would require new modes of marketing, advertising, automotive enticement. The cars might have small, slow engines, and might need to be used separately from over-powered conventional cars (because small cars in general fare badly in collisions with full-size cars). They would cost less to rent or to buy than conventional cars. But auto corporations, with their economic and managerial investment in upgraded marketing, might find themselves at a competitive disadvantage in such ventures, relative to other, nonautomotive companies. Such possible difficulties suggest the sort of interreacting problems corporations would face in transforming auto technology, the obsolescent "suitability" of production and work and selling. Technology is not an objective and mysterious force, but is the consequence, rather, of economic and historical changes—and there remains a sense in which contemporary auto technology, with its thousands of metal parts, is objectively anachronistic, and objectively difficult to change.

The troubles and inertia of auto technology form a gloomy pattern, affecting every aspect of auto manufacturing. This pattern, and the apparent inevitability of complex, unchanging auto production, will help to explain the behavior of auto managements. A last perspective on auto production comes from the attitudes of various groups of auto executives (who now seem a most beleaguered section of the managerial population: auto workers object not only to the repetition of jobs, but also to factory discipline, management attitudes, to the devaluation of work inherent in anachronistic auto manufacturing; the auto corporations are criticized by advanced business opinion on the grounds of inefficiency in production technology, and also in labor-management relations.)

The most famous of automotive poses is one of tough-mindedness. Severity has been since the time of Henry Ford a matter of automotive pride: and contemporary auto leaders still demonstrate the persistence of these Fordist beliefs. The opinions of these executives, expressed frequently in the business press, show the grossness of the inaction with which the modern auto business is sometimes possessed. It will also become clear that such attitudes are to some extent inherent in automotive organization, where the scientific management of work is supported by a scientific management of management.

But not all auto managers are ferociously Fordist. The GM labor relations experts I talked with in Detroit are aware of modern criticisms of automotive organization, and of Swedish, Japanese, and other foreign experiments in rearranging the repetitions of auto work. For these managers, a move towards programs for changing working conditions seems dictated by corporate self-interest. Yet it will be apparent that even conciliatory executives are troubled

by the same production problems that attend all auto operations—problems of trying to change technology (and work)
without fast industrial expansion, of trying to change the
value of work, of changing inherent management arrangements. Advanced auto attitudes may show, even more
clearly than corporate tough-mindedness, the force of automotive inertia.

Another business perspective on changes in work will
come from Mr. Fitzgerald, writing in the *Harvard Business
Review*. This Chevrolet executive, whose opinions are, according to the labor relations executives interviewed, heavily
unofficial, discerns yet further problems of industrial
change. He argues that the problem of "motivating" workers (to enjoy or tolerate work) has "roots" in "fundamental
conditions of industrial society"; that attempts to improve
jobs can, if intended seriously, damage management efficiency; and that corporations should anticipate a progressive deterioration of labor/management relations. This
argument amounts to a general critique of industrial job-
improvement projects—but the examples used have a particular relevance to automotive problems. From these examples, it will be possible to move, finally, to an evaluation of
the real prospects for automotive change.

The Tough-minded Executive

The highest auto executives determine the character of
much management comment. This comment is particularly
forthright when the executives discuss their own and other
automotive jobs. James Roche, for example, in a contempla-

tive interview given just before he retired as chairman of
GM, told the *Wall Street Journal* that "worker disenchant-
ment" had been "greatly exaggerated": "Too often all we
do is listen to the complainers and the growlers and the
trouble-makers. Hell, I can write a story about my own job
that could be a tear-jerker. You know, if all I want to do
is talk about all the problems and the pressures and the
monotony and the reading of all the reports you have to go
through. . . ." Lee Iacocca, president of Ford Motor Company, says that auto workers are "pretty well off, really. . . .
I don't say it's Utopia. But I don't go around saying 'Geez,
I'm sorry.' " Joseph Godfrey, of GMAD, expressed much
the same thought when he told one newspaper reporter that
"I don't think we have any more real work-related illness
now than we ever had. I have sinus, but it doesn't come
from my job." The Shelley Report has quoted the allegedly
idiosyncratic hope of an unnamed auto corporation's "training director" (who was probably a GM official, for he would
certainly approve of Mr. Godfrey's view, noted earlier, that
"workers like to do their jobs automatically") . He told the
interviewers that "it is not the repetition but the chaos
of the assembly process that is most discouraging, and [I]
would endeavor to maximize the sameness of workers' tasks
in order to increase job stability."

The world of the tough-minded executive can be summarized in Mr. Godfrey's corporate personality. Godfrey is
an enthusiastic proponent of reorganization and cost efficiency, and he also seems satisfied with the present conditions of automotive work. "In my opinion," he has told
Automotive News, "there is no such thing as monotony
on the assembly line any more than there is monotony in my

job"; he has also "suggested that the assembly line job is one of the best jobs in the industry and the auto industry compares favorably with other industries." "You can run an assembly line . . . so slow," he says, "that a man can't do his job right because he has his mind on other things." GMAD, under Godfrey, is engaged in developing training and orientation projects for its employees, yet Godfrey's personal view of production work seems best expressed in a comment he made to a *New York Times* reporter: "Within reason and without endangering their health, if we can occupy a man for 60 minutes, we've got that right." (Godfrey is the most purely Fordian of present auto celebrities. His enthusiam for the early Machine Age appears all-pervading. *Automotive News* points out, in a characteristically incisive profile, that "direct, friendly Joseph Godfrey" owns "what he calls a ranch up in Northern Michigan and he manages to get up there a half dozen weekends a year. 'I like to commune with nature,' he said. But just keeping the mechanical equipment of the ranch operating sounds like a considerable task. He operates a bulldozer, two tractors, a snowmobile, two boats, two Hondas and a trap range.")

Management "Fordism" is most stark when auto managers contemplate the character of work and workers. Yet these corporate attitudes reflect the conditions of auto production—and not only to the extent that they recall Henry Ford's bleakest pronouncements. There seems some inevitability about automotive tough-mindedness: if auto manufacturing is based at every phase on a precise and circumscribed use of unskilled work, m nagers are hardly likely to value such work. As at Lords town, the GMAD approach to discipline is less a matter of supervisory psychology than the result of scientific management techniques. GM's foremen are, in Alfred Sloan's military formulation, "our front line of supervision," whose salaries, since 1941, have "had to be at least 25 percent higher than the earnings of the highest paid group of employees under their supervision": the low status of production work is built in to all levels of company life.*

A fear of change seems inherent, also, in the organization of managerial and supervisory functions. Lordstown workers described how local foremen "want to get to be general foremen, up all the little steps of the ladder," and how each supervisor is under pressure from his superior, and his superior's superior; one worker said to me of GM that "they treat their own people worse than they treat some of us." Internal competitiveness is among the auto corporations' proudest boasts, and a major way in which they sustain their reputation for cost efficiency. Alfred Sloan's famous decentralization of GM's corporate organization was based on hierarchical competition, as found in modern auto factories. All GM managers must advance up the little steps of corporate evaluation; and all managers earning more than a certain salary are subject to the GM Bonus Plan, where they are "appraised" regularly, usually by their "immediate supervisors"; Sloan writes that "the knowledge

---

* When I first visited Lordstown, in 1970, I went to a mass meeting of the local union—then the largest ever held at Lordstown—where workers discussed the new truck plant. The biggest cheer came when one of the union officers said that the union would deal with management only according to the letter of the contract: "The last agreement I made with a clerk, I asked him to lend me a pencil—he told me to drop dead."

that his contribution to the corporation is weighed periodically, and a price put on it, acts as an incentive to each executive at all times." Sloan's principles of corporate free enterprise extended to matters of business strategy: he described, rapturously, "our tradition of selling ideas," and wrote that "The practice of selling major proposals is an important feature of General Motors' management. Any proposal must be sold to central management and if it affects other divisions it must be sold to them as well. . . . Central management should [also] in most cases sell its proposals to the divisions."

The present GMAD organization is the purest instance yet developed of Sloan's theory. In its rearrangement of assembly operations, the division is charged with rationalizing management as well as production. Mr. Godfrey believes that in his division "We probably have one of the most competitive organizations in the world." GMAD's eighteen plants, including Lordstown, are evaluated continuously and competitively; according to *The New York Times,* "There is a highly sophisticated (and computerized) reporting network, capable of giving Mr. Godfrey a daily performance rating for each plant. And, at the end of each month, each plant is ranked for efficiency and quality. . . . The ranking system is endless, since improvement in one plant pushes another down the scale." Such an organization has its own momentum of cost efficiency, which leaves little time for change, or for managerial contemplation. An official in the United Auto Workers' GM department described the GMAD program to me in the following way: "Each plant is evaluated every month, and whichever plant is

Number Eighteen, the manager is contacted. . . . It may be his cushion room [where seat cushions are made] is Number Eighteen of all the cushion rooms. This manager's Bonus is at stake, but if he pulls his plant around, then some other poor schmuck is Number Eighteen."

Competitive controls, as developed by Sloan and at GMAD, amount to a scientific management of management. Sloan helped to create an organization which was finely directed towards its goal of profitability and cost efficiency —and which was the brilliant completion of Henry Ford's achievement in organizing rationally the components and flows of auto manufacturing. Yet "rational" management attitudes now seem part of the auto industry's decline. They indicate, at least, the extent to which principles of cost efficiency and of restrictive work are inherent in company routines. The goal-directed precision of automotive organization has itself become a most solid factor in modern corporate immobility. Automotive inertia is weighted by fifty years of mechanical production—and by hundreds of thousands of intercorporate fears and submissions, from the Godfreys and Gerstenbergs to the "front line" of factory supervisors. (For present management theorists, such timidity seems regrettable. In *The Anachronistic Factory,* the Harvard business professor quoted earlier discusses the behavior of workers and managers in a factory designed according to criteria of cost efficiency—a factory that may or may not have automotive affinities. "Management Reactions" were represented as follows, in a scenario that seems more comical than profound:" Concern Hesitancy Paralysis Crisis Overreaction Piecemeal Syndrome ").

Moderate Opinions

Some company executives, even in contemporary U.S. auto corporations, would reject the most forthright comments of Joseph Godfrey. In the present situation of automotive labor relations, arguments for "flexibility" and for a modest "humanization of work" are likely to become increasingly compelling. The U.S. corporations have before them the example of flexible foreign auto manufacturers, all alarmed about labor unrest, and all mindful of long-term advantage: of Nissan's "quality circles" and of Volvo's and Saab's famous group production, with minimal assembly-line work; of Agnelli of Fiat, who soon after proposing that assembly-line jobs are "like knitting. If you break the monotony it can become more of a strain," emerged as an enthusiastic partisan of new working practices.* The apparently far-sighted GM executives to whom I talked in late 1972 had studied these foreign projects, and their comments reflect automotive attitudes to flexibility. These managers spoke candidly about the difficulties they anticipated— their remarks may perhaps explain, better than expressions of management tough-mindedness, the likely problems of automotive change.

The executives I met were concerned with the administration of personnel and "people." The discussion was led

---

* Nissan, producing Datsuns, uses "quality circles" of 7 or 8 workers, who discuss production efficiency. At Volvo and Saab, groups of workers assemble entire engines, change jobs often, and will soon, at a forthcoming Volvo factory, build entire cars without a final assembly line. Methods of group production are also used at Fiat—and at many non-automotive manufacturing companies in Japan, Europe, and the United States.

by GM's new vice-president in charge of personnel administration, Stephen Fuller, who had come to GM after a long
career at Harvard Business School. He explained that his
new department was intended to be "nonadversary," a
"people staff." Describing his colleague on the corporation's
industrial relations staff, he said "that vice-president is
always putting out a fire." His own department was more
contemplative: "GM's top management wants people innovations."

All the executives seemed to agree with Fuller's first
pronouncement, that present difficulties in automotive labor
relations were not "temporary or incidental." They agreed
that change in working relations was possible, and would
come about in different ways. Dr. Howard Carlson, one of
GM's behavioral scientists ("Behavioral science," he said,
"is on the increase in the corporation"), joined the discussion by saying that "most organizations have an objective
to survive," and that this is not enough. General Motors, he
added, now seeks corporate "progenitiveness," which he
explained was equivalent to "constant recycling" or
"growth and renewal."* None of the executives seemed
unduly respectful of Henry Ford's early work: Fuller said,
"Who was the industrial engineer? Frederick . . ." ("Frederick Taylor," says Carlson). "Well, that sort of thing can
lead to slicing of jobs." Everyone emphasized that many

---

* The concept of progenitiveness was explained further in a diagram
which I was given when I left GM. The diagram was called "a systems
model." Two concentric circles, the "organizational environment," were
surrounded by arrows. The circles enclosed two irregular hexagons,
around which was written " Individual Group Task Situation Structure Technology. " Inside the hexagons were more arrows, and, in a
box, the written word "progenitiveness."

different approaches to work must be examined. Fuller said
that "we don't want to concentrate on one gimmick," and
Carlson added that "to concentrate on one line, job enrichment, for example, is the same mistake as industrial
engineering."

GM, according to the executives, is now experimenting
with special training and participation programs, with
"complicating" jobs which had been simplified ten or
fifteen years before, and with training programs for foremen. Dr. Carlson said that "talking as a behavioral scien-
tist and not as a member of this corporation——" "You
can't," one of the other executives interjected. "Well, because as a representative of GM it would be boastful," he
continued, "there is nothing available in the field of the
behavioral sciences which is not being tried somewhere in
GM at the present time." The corporation was "keeping
abreast" of developments in automotive work at Volvo and
Saab, and had sent people to Sweden. One executive noted
that "many of the things they're doing [in Sweden] we're
already doing in the U.S.": none of the executives seemed
to agree with the comment of a Ford spokesman, that although the recent Swedish experiments were interesting, it
was still not necessary to "retreat full circle from the
pioneering work of Henry Ford." (Carlson also mentioned
that at future auto factories GM would "emphasize that
people are being put in proper perspective with machines
and bricks and mortar"; a components factory about to be
built in Jackson, Mississippi, would incorporate this principle, although on the basis of consultation with GM personnel administrators rather than with workers or unions at
existing factories.)

These remarks—although they were often quite abstract, and although the projects to which they alluded appeared somewhat tentative—expressed attitudes that were obviously different from those implied simultaneously by more prominent GM managers. Yet the GM executives also spoke revealingly about the problems of automotive change, in language that recalled the most general and recurrent troubles of auto production. They described problems of money and expansion, arguing that it was difficult to "tamper" with expensive investment, and to introduce new programs at old factories—Volvo and Saab, they said, had been able to build their innovations "around new factories." This difficulty has to do, evidently, with the long-term troubles of the U.S. auto business: with the economic lethargy of auto production and investment. New techniques for organizing work, like new technologies, are most easily applied in new plants, and Volvo, Saab, and Nissan have been among the most expansionary of international auto corporations.

Other problems concerned existing patterns of organization—and the management severity intrinsic to U.S. auto hierarchies. I asked the executives how GM's new and sometimes expensive training projects fitted with, for example, the rigorous systems of cost accounting used at GMAD, or with the GM Bonus Scheme. Fuller said that, eventually, "You [will] build into the reward system some reward for the manager who does a highly skilled job of utilizing people in his organization"; he gestured to Mr. Schotters, another participant who had risen from supervisor to plant manager to personnel administrator, and said, "Why is Frank Schotters sitting in this room with you? He was constructive and innovative." Mr. Crane, a participant from the "fire-fighting" Industrial Relations Staff, then said that there was "no correlation between training investment and the cost efficiency system." Dr. Carlson's answer to my question was to say that "It's inconsistent, isn't it."

A further problem discussed by the executives had to do with work—and reflected the devaluation of unskilled work inherent in auto production since the time of Henry Ford.* Mr. Fuller, discussing Schotters' training project, which had cost 25,000 "manhours," commented, as mentioned earlier, "Miss Rothschild, that has a hell of a price tag on it." Carlson asked whether workers really want change, and "does everyone have the skills to participate?" "What involvement do people want?" he asked, and Fuller noted that some workers will even say "I don't want to be foreman." These comments recall the Fordist assumption that many workers actually want bad jobs, jobs that are not only undemanding, or repetitive, but also overdisciplined and incomprehensible. Workers' "needs," on this assumption, are limited, intellectually, psychologically, morally: Carlson

* Another, mysterious, problem concerned the "character" of U.S. auto workers. Crane said, discussing European and Japanese work innovations, that for foreign auto manufacturers "problems are somewhat different." He mentioned "differences in mode of living," and in "ethnic background"; Carlson commented that in Sweden and Japan, "developments [in work organization] are coming out of the ideology of society." The only sense I could make of these remarks was that Swedish and Japanese societies were thought to be more cohesive than American society: that unregenerate auto work is particularly unpopular where workers, as in Sweden and Japan, are socially homogeneous, and highly educated. Neither Sweden nor Japan, for example, has a lavish "supply" of new and previously deprived native workers—the farmers, Appalachians, immigrants, blacks, Southerners and now perhaps women who have been hired successively as U.S. auto workers.

closed the discussion by warning that "sometimes, as behavioral scientists or as media people, we impose our own
needs on others." As far as automotive change is concerned,
the executives' remarks indicate that even in planning new
work projects, advanced auto managers face the general
troubles of auto production, and the general prejudices of
Fordist opinion.

Unofficial Pessimism

Beyond the problems discerned by Dr. Carlson and his colleagues, there remains a more general question about the
possibility and probable efficiency of projects to change
automotive work. Fitzgerald, the pessimistic GM executive
mentioned earlier, has addressed himself to this problem, in
an article called "Why Motivation Theory Doesn't Work,"
published in the *Harvard Business Review*. Fitzgerald, who
"was himself a first-line supervisor," is described as "Director of Employee Research and Training" at Chevrolet.
His argument proposes a general critique of motivation
theory and of job-improvement projects, but as a former
automotive supervisor he uses examples which apply in
particularly intense form to the auto business. (Fuller and
the other GM executives I talked with emphasized that the
Fitzgerald article was "not a corporate viewpoint." The
executives seemed uncomfortable when I mentioned the
article. Mr. Merriott, the generally taciturn representative
of GM public relations, said that the article was nonofficial;
Fuller said that he had not read the article; and Carlson

said that the published article had been given a wrong title, which Mr. Fitzgerald did not choose.)

For Fitzgerald, the "seriousness of the motivation problem has been underestimated." "In the business environment," he writes, "exchanging time for money may take care of a few of the worker's important needs, but it does nothing for ... other 'higher' needs." The problem of motivating workers is implicit in the "organization of rational work systems": in "stopwatch measurement," the replacement of "workmanship" by "machine process control," the "imperatives of short-range efficiency," the introduction of a "narrow division of labor." It is also related to "rational" and "objective" decision-making, and to the "spread of 'competitive' attitudes to the managers and supervisors of the work force." This description of the "factory system" has the most evident similarity to accounts of automotive organization; I asked Fuller about Fitzgerald's characterization of industrial life, and he said that "we are opposed to short range anything. . . . It is dysfunctional"—and added that "a short-term manager may spend [sic] part of the good relationships built up by his predecessor."

Fitzgerald speculates that workers may now seek "such intangibles and unbuyables as freedom and autonomy (one might add, following Baudelaire: beauty, clarity, luxury, and calm)," and comments, abruptly, that "These, obviously, are incompatible with the life of organized production." He argues that the three main recommendations of motivation theorists, "job enlargement," "training," and "participation," are incapable of resolving this contradiction. In another observation with clear relevance to the auto industry, he explains that attempts to change supervisory attitudes can be particularly troublesome—because the tendency of supervisors to be "bossy, condescending, and insensitive" may be the result of hierarchical "influences in the [corporate] organization." (Fitzgerald also comments that "the belief that a supervisor should be dominant, assertive, even truculent, is supported by a more general mythology of masculine authority and prowess, and by a leadership imagery borrowed from athletics and the military.")

The most dangerous of all motivation schemes is for Fitzgerald the "participation counsel." He argues that large organizations are so "linked, synchronized, interdependent," and the "store of knowledge" so "opaque," as to make participation impractical. ("It may in fact be true," he writes, "that the girls on the carton-folding operation really have nothing to contribute to almost anything important about running a container company.") His most serious argument against participation consists of a warning. Worker participation can be "dysfunctional" and "disruptive." Workers, when given some participation, may demand more. Modest and restricted participation may soon be "recognized by employees as manipulative or [may lead] to expectations for wider and more significant involvement." Workers consulted about "rearranging the work area . . . may very well want to go on to topics of job assignment, the allocation of rewards, or even the selection of leadership." "What is really involved," Fitzgerald writes, "is politics, the conscious sharing of control and power. History does not offer many examples of oligarchies that have abdicated with grace and good will."

The conclusion Fitzgerald draws from his gloomy argument is that motivation theories can be "subtly elitist," and can sometimes treat the "employee" as a "captive rodent." He seems to believe that some people cannot or do not want to be "motivated" at work, but he argues that serious change might require considerable expense, and a "relinquishing [of] certain behaviors and beliefs, such as an ideology of certitude and constraint, a habit of objectifying people because of ranking or role ascription." (His argument has been full of such contrasts: on the one hand, allusions to Baudelaire and to the "mythology of masculine authority"; on the other hand, mention of knowledge too "opaque" for "girls" folding cartons, and of the impossibility of Baudelairian freedom.) Fitzgerald provides no clear answer to management problems, but his main prediction is suitably somber (and relevant to the auto business): "Just as most of the signs point to a pervasive consumerism, environmentalism, and government surveillance in the market economy, so we should anticipate a persistent alienation of industrial and business manpower in respect to its employers."

Possibilities for Change

Automotive discontent is not new, but the conflict between peoples' expectations of what jobs should be like and the reality of auto production now seems more than ever intense. This conflict is unlikely to disappear, not only because of continuing changes in social expectations and aspirations, but also because automotive jobs compare increasingly unfavorably with jobs in other manufacturing and nonmanufacturing industries. Meanwhile, as at Lordstown, auto workers' discontent seems to go beyond the repetitive character of jobs to a rejection of management organization, factory discipline, the interchangeability and devaluation of work—conditions that are, as much as assembly-line monotony, an expected consequence of Fordist technology.

This complexity of discontent has grave implications for the possibility of automotive change, or, at least, for the possibility of change that will notably improve labor/management relations. If U.S. auto managements move away from the much criticized (and technologically limiting) GMAD efforts to increase organization and discipline, they seem likely to attempt the sort of training and "complication" projects mentioned by Dr. Carlson and his colleagues. One view of such change is provided by Chrysler, which is somewhat more adventurous than GM in altering production work, although its projects involve little open participation. The Chrysler executive in charge of job improvement told the *Wall Street Journal* that "there are people who think what I'm doing is dangerous, or kooky. But I tell them: Since we all agree the [traditional] system is failing, the only question is, 'How do you want to go down the drain?' "

Rearrangements in work might "enlarge" automotive jobs without improving the inherent management attitudes and structures which are a major cause of workers' discontent. If an alteration in working conditions becomes possible, auto corporations may face a further dilemma: on the one hand, improvements imposed by management may not be

q.

sufficient to deflect labor unrest; but on the other hand,
even if such improvements can deflect unrest, they may be
too extensive and costly for managements to tolerate. This
predicament recalls Fitzgerald's general critique of management "conciliation": in one of his long metaphors, "Participation especially ... not only may start out as an unpleasant ride for those who are accustomed to being fully
in charge, but also may become one from which it is
increasingly hard to dismount."

The difficulty of changing work seems particularly serious
for the auto industry, weighted by its fixation on early technology, on the consequent devaluation of work, on innate
management tough-mindedness. Companies that calculate
costs in manseconds are peculiarly unsuited to improving
working conditions—even though strikes and labor discontent can "waste" such "time resources," as GM found
at Lordstown, where enough production was lost, on management estimates, in the months of slow production which
preceded the 1972 strike, to use up all hoped-for savings
from assembly reorganization. Beyond their own inertia,
the corporations will face further and bitter problems of
social dissatisfaction. Leonard Woodcock, president of the
UAW, has criticized outsiders' accounts of auto work, saying, "Work is dull and monotonous. But if it's useful, the
people who do it are entitled to be honored and not degraded, which is what's going on in this day and time." Yet
a devaluation and degradation of work is implicit in the
structures of automotive organization—while the useful-
ness, if not the inevitability, of auto production is now itself
in question.

The present and expected conflicts of auto labor relations

are based on workers' rejection of automotive organization as well as of automotive tasks. The auto industry can anticipate that workers' attitudes will come to incorporate the more general repudiations of social criticism. To continue Fitzgerald's argument, workers might demand participation not only in "rearranging the work area" but also in decisions about how, and to what quality, automobiles are produced. Some Lordstown workers objected to GM's corporate organization and centralization, to the scheduling of long working hours, to management support for local garages, to the poor quality and expensiveness of Vegas. If automotive discontent is increasingly complex, the auto industry should expect that labor relations, like other automotive social relations, will come to reflect the declining glamour of massive auto corporations, of auto elaboration and costs and congestion—the complex of auto-industrial obsolescence.

6
Declines

The modern development of the automobile business suggests that auto domination faces at least a relative decline, in which its different problems react upon one another. Its troubles are based in historical change, and may be compared to the troubles of other industries, in other times— to the troubles of great aging industries of the past, and most particularly of the railroads and textile mills of late-Victorian Britain. The fate of these businesses shows a familiar pattern, whose failings include a fixation on the policies of a glorious past. Just as the modern auto corporations look back to the 1920s and 1930s, when Detroit seemed the capital of a mechanized world, so British industries of the 1890s mourned the 1840s and 1850s, and the supremacy of industrial Manchester.

The transformation of Detroit, from the 1930s to the 1970s, illustrates this comparison between the automobile business and other maturing industries in the history of world business. The now depressed romance of auto technology, and of industrial Detroit, was dominant in the same years as American auto selling. When the Italian car designer Pininfarina visited Detroit in the 1920s, he found "an earthly Paradise, the color of smoky gray"; Alfred Sloan, looking back at the early "evolution of the automobile," thought that "One of the striking scenes of America today viewed from the air in the daytime is the splash of jewel-like color presented by every parking lot."

In 1939 a most complete evocation of romantic Detroit appeared in *Life* magazine. In October of that year, for the first time, a Detroit girl was chosen as Miss America, and *Life* celebrated the occasion with an article about Detroit—"It Changed the World's Pattern of Life, and Is Now the Fourth City in the Land." Everything about Detroit was dynamic. "Half of Detroit works in factories," and half of the factory workers worked in automobile plants; Detroit was the "biggest purely industrial metropolis in the country." The city's business history was described concisely—a strategic location in the heart of American production, a supply of labor ("unskilled workers were drained from the farms around"), an industrial past ("long a manufacturing town, Detroit knew how to run machines when the auto-makers needed them").

Life's most euphoric comparisons were inspired by the Ford River Rouge plant, the "biggest industrial unit in the world." The factory had a "92-mile-long railway system," the "largest private power house in the world," "the largest foundry in the world," and "cleaning it, 5,000 mops and 3,000 brooms [were] worn out each month"; its "¼-mile-long motor assembly building" was "the world's number one shrine of Mass Production." Such superlatives were

applied to the social and cultural life of Detroit as well as
to its industrial power. The Detroit River was the busiest
waterway in the world. Hudson's department store in downtown Detroit owned the largest American flag ever made.
Detroit's own development was shaped by the automobiles
it "sent forth across the face of the earth." Even the traffic
was giant. "About half of Detroit drives to work in autos."
Traffic jams were an emblem of prosperity: "At 5:15 you
can almost hop across a street on the tops of cars frozen in
the traffic tie-up."

Auto selling was described in rapt detail as an essential
part of Detroit's supremacy. Fall, the time of the Miss
America contest, had a peculiar excitement for Detroit. It
was the season when the auto dealers of America made
their "annual pilgrimage to Detroit," to see "the new
Packards, Hudsons, Lincolns, Grahams, to see what
Chrysler had, what Ford was offering, what Harley Earl
has designed for General Motors. . . ." (Harley Earl, who as
a young man in Hollywood built custom automobiles for
movie stars, was GM's first Vice-President for Styling. By
1939 he was well advanced with his life's work, which he
summarized in 1954: "My primary purpose for twenty-
eight years has been to lengthen and lower the American
automobile, at times in reality and always at least in appearance.") The auto manufacturers advertised generously in
Life's Detroit issue, showing their more or less long and
low "offerings." A Ford advertisement expressed the spirit
of Detroit in 1939, when the Rouge plant was still a shrine,
and annual styling changes already romantic: "1940 Ford's.
Out of the World's Greatest Plant, THE NEW FORD CARS
ARE ROLLING."

Detroit never again reached the splendors of October 1939. The city's social organization—not as idyllic as *Life* had implied—was disrupted further by war production, and by the 1943 race riot. (*Life* wrote in 1939 that "looking across the Detroit River to a nation at war [Canada], the men of Detroit realize that if the war should come to America Detroit's super Mass-Production plant would become, in this age of mechanized battle, the backbone of the nation." "But," *Life* added, "their unanimous hope is for peace and boom times.") In the recessions and booms of the postwar auto economy, Detroit approached its present depression. The city followed the slow devaluation of automotive romance. Packard and Hudson, among *Life*'s auto makes, ceased operations and abandoned their Detroit auto plants. GM and Ford expanded auto production in rural and suburban Michigan, in Ohio and in other states far from the social tension of the country's "biggest purely industrial metropolis." In Dos Passos' *The Big Money*, published in 1936, "the stranger first coming to Detroit" finds "a marvelous industrial beehive," where "Detroit the dynamic ranks high."* By the 1970s, mechanical firms were leaving Detroit as fast as auto suppliers had arrived in the prewar booms. In a few weeks of 1972, for example, two machine-tool plants were moved from Detroit to western Michigan and Ohio, metal-spring operations moved to the South and to Canada, and the North American Rockwell

---

* Charley Anderson, hero of *The Big Money*, arrives in Detroit to work at the Tern Aircraft Corporation: "He had to get up and say how he was glad to get out there and be back in the great open spaces and the real manufacturing center of this country, and when you said manufacturing center of this country what you meant was manufacturing center of the whole bloody world."

Corporation decided to close an axle and forge plant it had operated in Detroit since 1912.

The city had become famous for its wide range of social privations, many of which reflected the auto industry's situation. For Jane Jacobs, Detroit was a model of cities which, concentrating on one industry, arrived at a "dead end." The General Motors Building on West Grand Avenue, a gold business cathedral, now stood in deserted gloom—recently, brightened only by the façade of an abandoned Hawaiian restaurant across the street, which had gone out of business, leaving behind its elaborate carved fountains. Ford planned to close, at last, its original auto factory in Highland Park; one of the GM public relations executives I saw in Detroit mentioned that many of his acquaintances now commuted from Dearborn to Warren (Michigan), or the other way around, living and working in different suburban cities outside Detroit. Hudson's department store was rumored each month to be on the point of folding its oversized flag and quitting the downtown city. The prosperous traffic jams of 1939 had turned bitter. A recent headline in the *Detroit News* proclaimed the "Detroit area worst in transit study"—that, according to a federal survey, Detroit was the only U.S. city (among the twelve largest) that "has done nothing tangible to develop a regional transportation system." The manager of the local Transportation Authority commented that "it's a pretty grim story": "Detroit has always been enamored of automobiles and freeways, and . . . we in Detroit have been the last to recognize their limitations."

The changes in Detroit's economic life suggest a process of industrial growth and decline hardly known in the

United States—of great cities developing and aging with
the fate of a particular industry. There have always been
municipal or regional victims of industrial obsolescence,
the towns along the Hudson which supplied ice to New
York City, or Danbury, a "Hat City" that outlived the
national demand for hats, or whole areas of industrial New
England. Yet the scale of decline now seen in Detroit goes
far beyond past American experience. A similar dislocation
can be found only in the cities of earlier industrial countries, in the cities, for example, of the English Midlands.
Jane Jacobs compares Detroit and Manchester, as cities
whose rise and fall were tied to the life of great national
industries: Manchester, a textile town in decline by the
1890s, and Detroit declining by the 1960s. A character in
one of Disraeli's novels said, in 1844, that "Certainly Manchester is the most wonderful city of modern times." Jane
Jacobs comments that "What impressed Disraeli, Marx,
and their contemporaries, and what made Manchester seem
to them—for better or worse—the most advanced of all
cities of the time, was the stunning efficiency of its immense
textile mills. The mills were Manchester. By the 1840s their
work dominated the city completely. Here, it seemed, was
the meaning of the industrial revolution, arrived at its logical conclusions. Here was the coming thing. Here was the
kind of city that made all other cities old-fashioned—
vestiges of an industrially undeveloped past." The implications of automotive decline go beyond Detroit, just as the
troubles of nineteenth-century British industries affected
the whole national economy; yet as centers of industrial
dislocation, Detroit and Manchester show the similarities
between British and American modern times.

Successive British businesses enjoyed the industrial and imaginative supremacy that the Detroit auto industry experienced in the 1920s and 1930s. The textile business, as in Manchester in 1844, seemed to epitomize the mechanization and the market expansion of the early Industrial Revolution: sixty years later, the British textile industry was troubled by foreign (including Japanese) competition, searched frantically for new markets, and was backward in applying the latest technology of automatic looms. The railroad business suffered a similar fall after its boom of the 1840s and 1850s, when rail magnates had displayed the same conviction of irresistible profitability, of power to change national destinies that Henry Ford and his contemporaries were to proclaim in 1920. The U.S. auto business now seems likely to follow the same historical course as these British industries—down to its present and expected troubles with slow growth, market saturation, management inertia, capital stagnation, technological demoralization. In Britain, around 1900, different industries reached what seemed like a climax of self-conscious discouragement. Contemporary observers ascribed the problems of the national economy to a lack of management dynamism, of "efficiency" (or productivity), of international vigor; historians have subsequently used the troubles of once great national businesses to explain the general decline of the British economy—describing what modern historians have called a "structural overcommitment to certain industries," or what Thorstein Veblen, writing in 1915, called an "inertia of use and wont," notably in railroad investment. There is no intention here to argue for the imminence of a general climax in American industry, or even of a climax in the older U.S. mass-production industries. The present concern is with the trajectory of the automobile business— and the early-twentieth-century troubles of specific British industries can go some way to explaining this historical path.

A hesitancy of business behavior was common to the industries participating in Britain's national crisis. E. J. Hobsbawm, describing the troubles of the late-nineteenth-century iron-and-steel business, writes that "Pioneer industrialisation (in a sector of economic development) created a pattern of both production and markets which would not necessarily remain the one best fitted to sustain economic growth and technical change. Yet to change from an old and obsolescent pattern to a new one was both expensive and difficult. It was difficult because it involved both the scrapping of old investments still capable of yielding good profits, and new investments of even greater initial cost." Inertia of this sort, in the depressed British Midlands as in modern America, has more to do with industrial history than with management psychology (although contemporary British observers lamented the fact that many iron industrialists came from a second or third, and effete, entrepreneurial generation—just as modern "administrative" U.S. managers are sometimes accused of lacking the feral energy of earlier mass-production entrepreneurs). Hobsbawm's pattern of industrial decline applies to several different British industries, each of which is similar in different ways to the U.S. auto business. Industries that enjoyed a rapid expansion in the mid-nineteenth century were by the end of the century growing less slowly, and were reluctant to make great capital commitments in an undynamic market. Foreign companies, with newer capital equipment, became increasingly competitive, while newer domestic industries inherited the romance of early industrial leaders. "Obsolescence" in production thus had two meanings, for British industries as for the U.S. auto business and its modern management critics: on the one hand, a failure to modernize technical processes as fast as in the past, or as fast as foreign producers; on the other hand, a commitment to an industrial sector which as a whole had passed its time of fastest growth.

The effects of productive obsolescence are illustrated by the British iron-and-steel and textile industries—both basic industries in the sense that steel was needed for almost all industrial expansion, while textiles were needed for the expansion of consumption. Hobsbawm shows that the British steel industry, whose production increased nearly four times over between the early 1870s and the early 1880s, and by little more than a half between the early 1890s and the early 1900s, was slow to adopt technological innovations. (In 1879, a Welsh police clerk, Gilchrist Thomas, invented a process for making steel out of low-grade iron ore, yet by 1913 less than one third of all British steel was made by his process.) Britain produced 40 percent of the world's steel in 1870, and about 10 percent by 1911; by the 1900s it had adequate industrial capacity, while the competitive and newer German and U.S. steel industries used more advanced capital equipment. The "scrapping [and replacement] of old investments" would have involved an expensive commitment to a depressed market: this self-reinforcing economic predicament was summed up by a Birmingham iron manufacturer who in 1904 told Joseph

Chamberlain's Tariff Commission investigating import restrictions that "We are so alarmed and disheartened at the approach of foreign competition that we fear to spend money [on new plants]."

Textile manufacturers showed the same pattern of industrial inertia. The early supremacy of Manchester industry was based on its productive equipment, on what the catalog of the 1851 Great Exhibition described proudly as the "iron arms and fingers" of cotton-making machinery. For one cotton entrepreneur of the 1850s, quoted by Hobsbawn, "self-acting (or automatic) machines . . . chiefly belong to Manchester, are of Manchester growth, and from Manchester they have had their origin." Yet by the 1890s British industries were slow to introduce newer automatic machinery, pioneered in America or France. The textile industry, alarmed by competition from India and Japan, bought little modern equipment even when its production expanded, although Lancashire machinery companies exported advanced machines to foreign producers. Textile manufacturers were prominent in late-nineteenth-century defensive chauvinism; the cotton business was also a favored target for the British "National Efficiency" enthusiasts of the 1900s, who, worrying about the "deterioration of the national physique," liked to point out that when 11,000 people in Manchester volunteered for the Boer War, 8,000 were turned away as physically unfit. A book called *Made in Germany* was published in 1896, listing German incursions into British daily and business life: the author quotes an opinion of the *Textile Manufacturer* magazine to the effect that "Turn whichever way we may, we are met with grimly significant indications that the condition of things is steadily going from bad to worse," and comments that "the Manchester man's commercial outlook is as gloomy as his native city," that he is obsessed with "political intrigue" against foreign rivals, while "[cotton] capitalists are getting to a condition of what is uncommonly like demoralisation."*

The strictures of such national pessimists extended to many British industries, and recall the most nerve-racked pronouncements of modern American executives, notably in the automobile, textile, and consumer electrical businesses. Germany assumed the position of inscrutable competitiveness now enjoyed by Japan, although the United States and Japan also appeared as formidable adversaries to early-twentieth-century Britain. (Americans were seen as adventurous, while one British national efficiency protagonist greatly admired the "organisation" and the "virile qualities" of the Japanese, and their "national capacity for self-reliant self-sacrifice.") *Made in Germany* urges the British reader to "roam the house over" and note how many of his possessions are stamped with "the fateful mark" that provides the book's title. The author argues for trade protection and for national regeneration, but accepts economic explanations for much of Germany's success. German goods were not, for example, as commonly supposed, "cheap and nasty"; it was also "a great mistake" to assume that "the cheaper pig iron to which the Germans now have access is inexpensive solely by reason of low wages. The better explanation is to be found in the increased productivity of the German furnaces." Some of the

---

* The author's other works include a volume called *The Foreigner in the Farmyard*.

psychological and political observations in the book are most surprisingly familiar. German progress is attributed to the absence of strikes, the "greater steadiness of the German worker," to the German "faculty of imitativeness," to "State Help" in "Protection," domestic "Bounties and Subsidies," "Commercial Consuls" in foreign export markets; to the fact that German entrepreneurs try harder, never "neglect the wishes of foreign customers," learn "the language of the country which they are to canvass," and generally express "an alert progressiveness, contrasting brilliantly with the conservative stupor of ourselves."

Made in Germany achieves a style of masochistic rhetoric not reached by even the most demoralized of U.S. commentators, and American industrial troubles are much more limited than those of the late Victorians. Yet certain modern observations approach this style: the opinion of "29 machine tool corporations," advertising in the *Wall Street Journal,* that "American industry has the highest percentage of over-age, obsolete production facilities of any leading industrial nation"; the words of James Roche, of GM, who has told the California Chamber of Commerce that U.S. labor relations compare most unfavorably with labor relations in Japan and Germany, that there are too many strikes in the United States, and that the United States should emulate competitor nations and undertake a "careful revaluation of our [labor] system"—and who has urged, elsewhere, that "We must work, and work hard, if we are to counter this challenge [from other industrial countries]. . . . We must somehow muster a great national effort that involves the entire citizenry." One modern historian of the early-twentieth-century "Ideology of National Efficiency" writes that for British pessimists "the key to the internal policy of the German Empire was 'this central idea of national efficiency,' just as the key to British national life was to be found in 'the idea of personal liberty.' " These and other descriptions of international development could stand unamended in contemporary accounts of "Japan Inc."—with its disciplined work force, singing company songs, stealing markets, and striving for a productive future.*

Of all the industries that participated in the late-Victorian decline of British business, the railroad business had the closest and most premonitory resemblance to the modern auto industry. The situation of the railroads, like that of American auto-industrial business, was based on a once glorious arrangement of technology and markets—and also on an unprecedented complex of social and political power. (No Victorian industries, of course, enjoyed the benefits and complexities of developed consumer marketing—a sort of marketing which was refined only with the growth of the automobile industry itself.) The British iron-and-steel

---

*For some Europeans, at the time of Fordist supremacy in the 1920s and 1930s, American society seemed to possess the productive coherence ascribed by the British to the Germans, and by Americans today to the Japanese. The Italian socialist Antonio Gramsci, in an early-1930s essay on "Americanism and Fordism," noted this American discipline, and commented that in the United States "it was relatively easy to rationalize production and labor by a skillful combination of force . . . and persuasion (high wages, various social benefits, extremely subtle ideological and political propaganda) and thus succeed in making the whole life of the nation revolve around production. Hegemony here is born in the factory." This explanation of national persuasion suggests that social and worker cohesiveness has more to do with a generalizable pattern of industrial history than alarmed commentators might allow, in the United States today, or in Britain in 1900. National efficiency, as a quasi-moral force, is related to rapid industrial growth, as well as to racial or patriotic peculiarities.

industries displayed the same pattern of technological maturity that now troubles the auto industry, but their marketing problems had more to do with export selling and foreign competition than those of the modern auto business—the chauvinism of iron and textile magnates was perhaps more rational than Henry Ford II's now seems. The railroad industry's domestic market, by contrast, was limited in much the same way as the modern auto market: Britain was covered with railroad lines, whose development had determined the shape of national life, of cities, suburbs, farms, factories, family histories. Like automotive capital, railroad investment seemed immovable, a fact of contemporary society. The inertia of the railroad business was inherent in political groupings as resolute as the modern highway lobby, and in iron tracks as tangible, and relatively as expensive, as the concrete of the U.S. Interstate Highway system. Railroad decline, more than that of any other industrial sector, can help to explain the auto industry's present history—and can indicate some of the dislocations to be expected in the automotive future.

The railroad boom of the 1840s and 1850s expressed, as much as Manchester textile automation, the romance of mid-Victorian technology. Hobsbawm describes the "acute, even irrational joy in technical progress" that characterized early railroad building; he writes that " 'railway' became a sort of synonym for ultra-modernity in the 1840s, as 'atomic' was to be after the Second World War," or as "mass production" was in the 1920s. Railroad capital increased many times over in the 1840s alone, and railroad shares were responsible for the early success of the London stock market. Giant fortunes were made by rail magnates and by financial speculators. In the "Railway Mania" of the mid-1840s, as a later Victorian described it, railway fever was "not confined to the precincts of the Stock Exchange, but infected all ranks," and "many persons utterly ignorant of railways, knowing and caring nothing about their national uses, but hungering and thirsting after premiums, rushed eagerly into the vortex." Infected perhaps by the romance of railroads as well as by a thirst for profit, these early Victorians made money out of the railroads; rail capital doubled again between 1850 and 1870, as did the mileage of national railroad tracks. This early combination of profitability and technological joy was matched in more recent times only by the (shorter, and more abruptly ended) Wall Street boom of the 1920s—a bull market that was sustained by auto stocks, and where the "Four Horsemen" of the boom were General Motors, Fisher Body, Du Pont, and Yellow Cab.

Beyond its productive force, the railroad business seemed marvelous for its power to change national life. The early rail inventors and entrepreneurs felt the same confidence in their ability to improve societies that Henry Ford expressed when he wrote, "We have remade this country with automobiles," or that was implicit in *Life's* description of the cars that Detroit "sent forth across the face of the earth," or that a Cadillac tycoon felt in 1915 when he predicted that automobiles would increase "in number and utility until they cover the face of the earth." One of the most widely read of all Victorian books was a biography of the rail inventor George Stephenson, in Samuel Smiles's famous series *Lives of the Engineers*. The main theme of the book is Stephenson's perseverance and dedication in adversity to the ideal of a "railway system" that would benefit the "working man." Stephenson was able to die happy, largely because he had seen the London-to-Birmingham railroad: a construction which for Smiles exceeded the Great Pyramid of Egypt by around 250 percent in "magnitude" and which displayed most clearly "the levelling tendencies of the age" (as explained by Matthew Arnold's father, who, according to Smiles, stood on a railway bridge over the Birmingham line, watching the trains and saying, "I rejoice to see it, and to think that feudalism is now gone for ever.") *

The early railroad civilization seemed no less irrevocable than modern automotive arrangements. Railroads, like highways, changed cities and created suburbs—and like highways they were praised with statistical anthems. In an introduction, written in 1879, to his life of Stephenson, Samuel Smiles recalls that people once opposed the railroads: "But such nonsense is no longer uttered. Now it is the city without the railway that is regarded as the 'city lost'; for it is in a measure shut out from the rest of the world, and left outside the pale of civilization." Among the achievements of the British railway system, Smiles notes a 300 percent increase in the size of London,

* Friedrich Engels, in 1844, looked at railroad construction in another way, much as modern observers see the urban expressways carved through poor neighborhoods of Oakland or Boston: "The narrow side lanes and courts of Chapel Street, Greengate, and Gravel Lane [in Manchester] have certainly never been cleansed since they were built. Of late, the Liverpool railway has been carried through the middle of them, over a high viaduct, and has abolished many of the filthiest nooks; but what does that avail? Whoever passes over this viaduct and looks down, sees filth and wretchedness enough."

the "rapid growth of suburban towns up and down the [Thames]," the provision of many thousands of trains to accommodate the "vast traffic" of London, "in the morning hours, between 8.30 and 10.30, when businessmen are proceeding inwards to their offices and counting houses." By the 1870s, 450 million people were carried on the railways each year: "It is difficult to grasp the idea of the enormous number of persons represented by these figures. The mind is merely bewildered." In 1867, Smiles writes, the railroads delivered to London 1,147,609 sheep, 11,259 tons of French eggs, and 1,250,566 sacks of flour, while one small line imported 5,000 tons of broccoli, and the Camden Town railroad station handled up to 20,000 parcels a day.

It is exactly this sort of calculation with which modern fatalists—or enthusiasts—explain the inevitability of auto and truck transportation. Like the railroads, automotive civilization is weighted by the inertia of broccoli and suburbs. The author of a recent study, *The Road and the Car in American Life,* describes American society in 1967: with 733,542 gas station employees, and 51,353 motels and trailer parks employing 242,821 people; where trucks delivered to Los Angeles 2,266 hauls of cabbage (a haul being the equivalent of a car-lot), 11,276 hauls of potatoes, 1,829 hauls of green corn, or 97 percent of all the green corn eaten in Los Angeles. Where "the record of passenger-miles and vehicle-miles accumulated in highway travel reveals a drama of mobility difficult to describe in its totality . . . but significant and stimulating"; where the "suburban explosion" of society was "automobile-based," and where suburban dwellers "are looking for open space and a sense of community that the impersonality of the great city does not provide"; where automobiles made possible a freedom of religious "choice," by encouraging drive-in churches, and where the U.S. Interstate Highway system was an achievement comparable only to the road-works of the Roman Empire.

Like Victorian railroads, U.S. automotive power created the institutions and the suburbs that support its growth. Like railroad power, it was sustained by social enthusiasm and by government partiality: by the complex of highway favor which sanctioned, among other benefits, the use of automotive taxes for building new highways, the use of scarce land for building low-density suburban housing, the use of city streets for free parking, the subsidy of trucking by taxing highway freight transportation more favorably than rail or pipeline transportation, the destruction of urban bus transport as buses and their passengers suffocated on streets and in driving lanes congested with private, half-empty automobiles.

In Britain, after 1850, the national economy was built around the railroads—in an organization of society supported by the powerful political group of "railway interests," watching fiscal and statutory regulation of the industry, and guarding the monopolies of different rail companies. Yet by 1900 the railroad industry faced a situation of economic decline. It had invested about as much money during the 1890s as it had in the 1860s, although national investment had doubled. The number of passengers carried on the railroads was growing more and more slowly, as was the mileage of tracks open; profits fluctuated depressingly. The major recent achievements of British rail engineers had been in the Empire and the tropics. For the author of *Made in Germany*, the monopolistic, inefficient, and not notably profitable "railway system" was an important cause of British industrial decline. Few people, in 1900, believed that the railway system could be changed (when the British Parliament in 1896 passed its famous law allowing automobiles to use public roads without being preceded by a man with a red flag, representatives roared and laughed at the suggestion of one politician that "it was even possible that these motor cars might become a rival to light railways"). But the early glamour of the rail companies had disappeared: the electrified London underground railway was built in the 1900s—with largely American equipment, and largely foreign capital.

Pessimistic British commentators had come to understand some of the disadvantages of early industrialization, and of the mid-century railway boom. British railroads, with their beautiful and elaborate stations, were often more expensive than foreign lines, while the free enterprise of different rail companies led to riotous inefficiency. More generally, the Edwardians began to perceive the extent of the nation's "structural overcommitment" to railroad transportation. (Hobsbawm argues that capital in the early rail boom was "rashly, stupidly, some of it insanely invested," and that many of Britain's transport needs could have been served more rationally by water transport, on the seas and rivers, and on existing canals. Similar arguments apply to the present situation of transport economics. Much heavy freight can be moved more efficiently by train than by truck—yet railroads are now thought to be an archaic form of transport, as eighteenth-century canals were in the 1840s.)

The theory of Britain's historical decline, and of the immobility of national investment, was expounded as early as 1915, by Veblen. Comparing Britain disadvantageously with "Imperial Germany," Veblen argued that nations which first approach "modern times" are likely to develop an "interdependence" of economic life, an "inertia of use and wont" which may prevent further industrial growth. Veblen's major examples of this effect are taken from the British railways. He mentions such blatant but intractable irrationalities as the size of the British rail gauge, which was several inches smaller than newer foreign gauges— "The remedy," he writes, "is not a simple question of good sense. The terminal facilities, tracks, shunting facilities, and all the ways and means of handling freight on this oldest and most complete of railway systems, are all adapted to the bobtail car." His gravest explanation has to do with the structure (or what modern auto commentators might call the "infrastructure") of the national economy, and of rail investment. The displacement required to modernize industry would not be easy: "Towns, roadways, factories, harbors, habitations, were placed and constructed to meet the exigencies of what is now in a degree an obsolete state of the industrial arts." Veblen's arguments cannot explain the general history of the British economy, far less of other economies. Yet the inertia he described may be found in many industrial sectors—in the British railroad industry, and in the modern U.S. auto and highway business. Veblen's harbors and habitations are the same structures that Samuel Smiles so admired, in his hymn to the social power of the railway system, and they represent the same immobility that has weighted successive international industries, in their decline.

The troubles of the modern auto business have the most evident resemblance to the troubles of mature British industries—problems of a fixed technology and of fixed markets, as with the steel and textile industries, and problems of structural inertia, as with the railroads. The national investment that supported "obsolete" industrial arts and inefficient railroads was the same sort of investment that sustains present automotive power: the urban and social and fiscal development that makes it rational for Americans to buy cars, because jobs and schools and supermarkets are accessible only by highway. George Stephenson, who died in 1845, hoped that the British "working man" would one day be able to travel by train as cheaply as he could walk. His ideal had been achieved by 1900—but for some workers train commuting was now compulsory, as jobs became dispersed around the great cities. The same lack of choice characterizes modern automotive freedom, as alternative means of transport vanish, and as the automobile becomes a necessity of life, or of earning and spending money.

The inertia of social rationality is the basis of modern auto-industrial power, as it was the basis of the railroads' power. Like rail power in 1900, automotive arrangements now seem superhuman and perpetual. Yet the experience of the British railways may provide some idea of likely future changes, as it has of past and present auto troubles. Thousands of miles of British railroad track are now grassed over, battered, and abandoned—the victims, in fact, of a later British overcommitment to highway transportation, notably more insane than the early railroad boom. Interstate highways are less easily grassed over than rail tracks. But it does not seem inconceivable to anticipate some similar, and similarly long-term, reduction in the American automotive system.

The "crisis" of 1900, although perhaps more apocalyptic in speculation than in economic reality, and although it was concentrated in certain old-established sectors of the national economy, disappeared only with the most radical transformation of British industry. Britain is still an industrial nation, and still produces steel and textiles—but at the expense of a traumatic displacement of people, jobs, factories, cities, capital. Business can overcome the immobility inherent in old industrial arrangements: in Britain, as in other industrial countries after 1900, the technologically newer chemical and electrical industries expanded while older businesses declined; and by the 1920s and 1930s, for example, the British mass-production auto industry enjoyed reasonably booming times. But this survival of the national fittest, similar to the readjustment now developing between the U.S. auto industry and newer, service, or plastic-based industries, was notably less agreeable for the people who lost 160,000 jobs in the cotton industry between 1923 and 1929 than it was, for example, for the city of Coventry, where, according to Hobsbawm, "textiles went down after 1860, but the local watch-makers became the nucleus of the bicycle industry, and through it later of the motor industry."

The American auto industry may be able to emulate the economic flexibility of declining British businesses—and the general situation of the U.S. economy is less distressed than that of the British economy, in 1900 or subsequently. Yet any possible auto adjustments will involve dislocation, of people and cities, and of business psychology. The

British experience suggests two main, and similarly disruptive, paths of change. The auto corporations can attempt to increase domestic productivity by reorganizing their production and markets: by struggling against the basic technology of auto manufacturing, or by producing new sorts of goods—from simple or clean cars to recreational vehicles to mass-transit systems to transportation "services." They can also increase or accelerate their foreign auto and auto-component production. This possibility, like the possibility of domestic transformation, was available to British entrepreneurs: Friedrich Engels wrote in 1885, in an essay called "Britain in 1845 and 1885," that "new markets are getting scarcer every day, so much so that even the Negroes of the Congo are now to be forced into the civilization attendant upon Manchester calicos, Staffordshire pottery, and Birmingham hardware."

The last parts of this book will examine these different automotive hopes, and the problems they may entail. Domestic readjustment could involve the auto corporations in the dire struggles of productivity that determine the survival of the industrial fittest; foreign expansion may bring intensified competition with Japan and other industrial producers, and will meet the evident difficulties of forcing such countries as Turkey, Rumania, and the Philippines into the "civilization attendant upon" highways, accessories, and second cars. The past of the U.S. auto business followed a familiar historical path: it now remains to look at the more or less encouraging possibilities of the automotive future.

7

New Ventures

Industrial evolution is a history of cruel fates. In the rise and fall of international businesses, some industries are victims, along with their factories and workers and managers. In Darwin's theory of biological evolution, as species failed, dinosaurs or ground sloths, Natural Selection tended to "progress towards perfection." Capitalist Darwinism can expect no end in the efficiency of *Homo sapiens*: industrial species are fated to boom and die perpetually, as business evolves from one need to the next. The argument of this book has been that the American automobile business, which in the 1920s and 1930s was an international survivor, now faces decline and possible extinction—a decline that can be seen most clearly in the continuing readjustment of modern American and world industries.

The process by which the industrial fittest survive moves capital across countries and continents, back and forth across the world, into one industry and out of another. In the United States, older consumer-goods industries lose capital to industries offering services, utilities, social goods; the low-technology and mass-production industries lose capital to high-technology or research-based industries. In the world market, low-technology and labor-intensive industries move to ever less developed countries, with low-paid workers: assembly technology was a growth area for U.S. business in the 1930s, for Japan in the 1960s and early 1970s, for South Korea and the Philippines, perhaps, in the 1980s and late 1970s. Some patterns of declining British industry obtain today. The United States, like Britain in the 1910s, retains world leadership in the most advanced science, and in heavy armaments— and as British textile capital and world textile leadership moved from Manchester to India and Japan, so U.S. capital in lower-technology industries moves to Japan, Korea, the underdeveloped world.

Such national and international readjustments are anticipated eagerly by advanced American business opinion, by partisans of financial corporations and of the more dynamic and science-based multinational companies. The *Wall Street Journal* has described editorially its vision of future business, where the United States will concentrate on high-technology industries selling, for example, computers, mass transit, pollution control. U.S. corporations will export money and technological expertise, while "less developed nations" will attract less advanced industries. The harsh but bracing result of such an adjustment will be that "some companies won't survive, but new ones will arise. Some workers and executives will find their old skills outdated and will have to learn new ones." *Fortune* in 1971 de-

scribed a similar scenario of free trade and free competition: it argued that the United States still enjoyed basic
and profitable advantages in technology, business organization, foreign policy, and the generation of capital;
dismissing the fears of (by implication, low-technology,
obsolescent, and vulgarly protectionist) automotive chau-
vinists, it wrote that "An American who understands these
strengths will hardly panic about Toyota's U.S. sales
figures."

This vista of industrial rearrangement is expressed in
another metaphor of advanced business thought. *Fortune*
explains world trade relations in terms of the war games
of uneven development: "If one line of products is forced
to retreat in the face of competition, the only hope may
be that another line will advance." The American auto
industry now seems a business facing retreat, from the
competition of newer U.S. industries, and of more newly
industrialized nations. The struggles of industrial survival
explain not only the possibilities of auto change but also
the general adjustments of domestic productivity—not only
international automotive competition, but also the likely
course of world industrialization.

The present national preoccupation with productivity
goes beyond industrial statistics to an abstract anxiety
about American dynamism—and the auto business, as an
industry moving from advance to demoralization, is prominent in such anxiety. The word "productivity" has the
same connotation for some modern American politicians as

"efficiency" had for the British National Efficiency movement of the 1900s. Like efficiency, productivity is the object of exhortations and random investigations. Blame is distributed as indiscriminately for failings of productivity as it was for failures of efficiency: such failures are the fault of national complacence, of business conservatism, of workers' laziness, of strikes, of antitrust laws, of government failure to support national technology, of management chauvinism. The main national apostle of productivity, Peter Peterson, who is one of President Nixon's economic advisers and a former Secretary of Commerce, sounds sometimes like a most promising disciple of the British ideology of moral hygiene—as when he calls for a "comprehensive national crusade" to increase productivity.

When he was Secretary of Commerce, Peterson wrote to the *Wall Street Journal* that productivity growth is "the key to our economic strength and national survival," noting gloomily that between 1965 and 1970 productivity grew more than nine times as fast in Japan as in the United States, and that the United States had the lowest rate of growth of productivity of any "developed nation in the free world." The National Commission on Productivity, sponsored by Secretary Peterson, in 1972 began a "public education program" to explain productivity through advertisements and inspirational slogans. President Nixon reminded citizens that America was no longer a "sort of technological cornucopia." Scientists, like managers and workers, were urged continually to undertake an extra effort for national efficiency; presidential messages to Congress promised "Research and Development Prizes," and a "New Technology Opportunities Program," to be directed by the former manager of the supersonic transport (SST) project. Automotive executives participated enthusiastically in these discussions, Iacocca of Ford lamenting the crisis of domestic dynamism, and Roche of GM calling for a great national effort.

The American debate about productivity used language of often extreme abstraction, yet like earlier British debates, it also corresponded to real changes in the national economy. Beyond the distribution of slogans and prizes, discussions of productivity raised the most serious questions of industrial readjustment, between high and low technologies, new and old markets. The industries that received political approval were, usually, those science-based businesses designated by *Fortune* or the *Wall Street Journal* as the modern fittest. Other businesses could expect an opposite fate. Secretary Peterson has classified American industries into a (fast) "technology-intensive" group making computers, aircraft, pharmaceuticals, and a (slow) "non-technology-intensive" group making textiles, footwear, paper, with the auto business assigned a questionable status: in the productivity debate, the auto industry with other businesses of dubious technology faced the accumulating horrors of slowly growing productivity, slowly changing products, slowly stagnating markets.

The causes of economic distress, in the United States as in early-twentieth-century Britain, are to be found not in national psychology but rather in the troubles of distinct industrial sectors. The productivity crisis is about the fate of specific industries. Some businesses in the "fast" group of American industries prospered through the bleakest days of the uncompetitive late 1960s, ignoring the troubles of national morale. Other industries were afflicted simultaneously with all the different failings mentioned in political exhortations—with failings in selling, efficiency, business morale, scientific research, labor relations.

The recent crisis of U.S. productivity does not equal the climactic force of earlier British crises, except in national rhetoric; the dynamic sector of U.S. business is notably more dynamic than its early-twentieth-century British counterpart. Yet the general troubles and readjustment of U.S. business can provide the context for the present problems and changes of the automobile business. Like the troubled British railroad and textile industries, the auto business can prosper only by changing its strategies; like these industries it must achieve such change in the permanent competition of national industrial adjustment.

The inertia described throughout this book also afflicts other industries. The auto industry still feels only indirectly the extent of its fall from past glories; it has yet to contribute its full economic weight to national economic crisis. In the years of slow growth decried by Secretary Peterson, the auto industry fared worse than in previous decades, but remained at the center of the national productivity league. Yet its troubles of marketing and production are exactly the sort of troubles that characterize industrial obsolescence generally. Nostalgic auto executives lament foreign competition, consumer discontent, government regulation; Joseph Godfrey of the General Motors Assembly Division, pondering the difficulties of organizing auto work, tells *Automotive News* that "I'm not a prophet of doom, but I think the productivity problem is worse than it seems."

All industries confront similar sorts of problems in their search for productivity. To survive the struggles of industrial readjustment, business, including the auto business, must alter its markets and production. In the vigorous vocabulary of business approval, the highest qualities, beyond even "dynamism" and "resolution," are "flexibility," "willingness to change," "future-orientation." The essential business objective is to sell new things, made in a new way. Such adaptability can be found in many different industries, yet with certain common attributes. Survivors must conform to a model of successful business Darwinism, perpetually encouraging new ventures and extinguishing others, hoping perpetually that some new species will be the gunpowder or the nylon of the technological future.*

* The auto companies, with their historical commitment to one industry and one restrictive technology, are among the least keen of all large corporations in attempting new ventures. Corporations in the petroleum and chemicals businesses, and other companies which use much capital and research, or which are already diversified, seem relatively eager: a *Wall Street Journal* survey of "venture capital" found Exxon investigating computer speech, Dow Chemical involved in medical X-rays and Alaskan housing, and General Electric investigating computer speech and artificial kidneys. Du Pont's recent history can illustrate the required behavior for "dynamic" industrial survival. Du Pont and GM grew together, were organized similarly, and were linked financially and economically for much of their history; as a chemicals corporation, Du Pont participated in major research and development advances of the 1940s and 1950s, in the continual transformation of modern chemicals, and in the continuous-process production of the 1950s. In the late 1960s Du Pont fell on bad times, yet now appears as a hero of business evolution. It sells new products, from pharmaceuticals to electronic equipment, and it sponsors new, improved technologies. The restyled Du Pont is described eulogistically in the business press as "ruthless" and "streamlining," closing plants and divisions and cafeterias, an example of "flexible, resolute" management, which can, repulsively enough, "sweat out" its fat. The corporation is said to be "productivity-minded": it now offers X-ray equipment, electronic and automatic machines for testing blood and analyzing medical data, instruction services for schools and prisons.

Industrial adjustment is Darwinian in its power to destroy ventures, yet it is also arbitrary in its selection of new business species. It has no end; it learns no lessons. Businesses thrive or survive through a complex endowment of qualities and opportunities, and classifications of industries into "fast" and "slow" are only approximate. Industrial modernity is related to capital intensity and to scientific advance, and these in turn are related to historical movements, such as, perhaps, present moves from mass-production consumer markets to those markets for services and social goods where businesses employ technical rather than unskilled workers: it can at the same time seem random and irrational, demanding only disruption.

With no end beyond permanent change, business evolution creates odd and anachronistic mutations. Though the modern automobile industry must change its markets and its production, its old strategies recur, for the benefit of newer industrial groups. Methods of Fordist technology, so troublesome for present auto corporations, are used enthusiastically in other industries. The techniques for regulating work, which Marx observed in early British textile factories, and which Henry Ford applied to unskilled work in twentieth-century assembly plants, are now being attempted, for example, in an effort to control the jobs of office and technical and service workers. A *Business Week* survey of national productivity discovered the automation of supervisory work at a Westinghouse factory that builds equipment for power-generating plants, where computers "send an assignment to a production worker via a teletypewriter." It also investigated service companies, and found that "Budgeting and financial controls, time-and-motion studies, and standardization and specialization are appearing in everything from lawn care to repair work to advertising."

For some service and nonmanufacturing industries, Fordist reorganization can be a most modern means of increasing productivity, of changing the ways in which services are produced. *Fortune,* for example, reassures executives that improving productivity need not be expensive, and that "a lot can be done just by applying basic techniques of industrial engineering more rigorously." It describes the possibilities for a Fordist intensification of white-collar work, as explained by a modern industrial consultant named Joseph Quick. This Frederick W. Taylor of the filing cabinet "begins by measuring the average amount of time necessary to perform various low-level mental functions [such as the jobs of "salesmen, draftsmen, office workers, etc."]. In general, Quick says, people don't mind working harder." But such refinements are not available to auto corporations themselves. As a pioneer of time-study methods, the auto industry is badly placed to participate profitably in the anticipated regulation of U.S. labor. It employs large numbers of unskilled workers whose jobs have been subjected to such regulation for at least fifty years: it has already applied the basic techniques of industrial engineering with incomparable rigor; in Fordism, it has nowhere left to go.

Like other industries, the auto business could survive and change, in the ways described below—yet the mutually reinforcing power of market inertia, Fordist mass production, and management demoralization will affect even the bravest of auto opportunities. Auto companies will certainly attempt new American ventures in the next decade, ventures which will alter both selling and technology. But these attempts, though they will determine the future of the auto business, will evolve from present troubles of auto selling and productivity—and from present difficulties of national economic adjustment.

Safer and Cleaner Cars

The most immediate opportunity for automotive expansion comes from public and political concern about making cars safer and less polluting. The auto corporations have been slow to acknowledge the business advantages of consumer activism; yet certain consumer demands suggest a profitable new mode of product improvement. Auto history consists of the search for newer and more irresistible auto options, newer and more lucrative upgradings. As the market for conventional accessories becomes less promising, auto manfacturers may be able to sell new kinds of safety improvements at higher and higher prices. Instead of being faster each year, more comfortable, or more beautiful, cars could each year be, or seem, cleaner and safer.

Late-model automobiles already show signs of hesitant corporate "consumerism": 1973 Vegas are advertised as enjoying the "safety of a side guard beam in each door"; many automobiles are available with an optional "special [safer] handling package," and *Motor Trend* equips one of its test Pintos with a $60 option described as a "protection group." The president of GM, Edward Cole, has told the National Automotive Parts Association, optimistically, that

government enforcement of safety and antipollution regulations "may create pressure for customer maintenance that
may encourage more parts sales." (Datsun, without yet
offering antiemission auto accessories, has mounted a most
successful advertising campaign on the theme of "Datsun
Is Greening America." Advertisements urged "Drive a
Datsun—Plant a Tree," and claimed "It's the truth. From
little Datsuns mighty trees do grow." The company promised
to plant a tree in a national forest whenever a customer test-
drove a Datsun: advertising representatives say that the
campaign "really hit a nerve" among the environmentally
concerned.)

Mandatory auto improvements, which inspire the worst
rage of the U.S. auto corporations, will be sold at federally
controlled prices. Yet even were the auto companies to
show a loss on the sale of such devices, federal regulation
of automobiles could encourage some upgrading of the auto
market, as people decide to buy safer or cleaner cars, with
new options to improve upon (or compensate for) mandatory equipment. A financial analyst specializing in auto
shares has spoken most euphorically about the prospects
for selling clean new engines, such as, perhaps, Wankel
rotary engines: "The new engine or power plant could be
a hypo to the business, as people who might not have
bought a [new] car race out to get the new thing. If a new
power supply will make every car on the road obsolete, the
natural consequence will be to accelerate scrappage." The
new markets, as Cole told the auto-parts makers, can
benefit independent auto suppliers, including firms supplying equipment for Wankel engine production, or metals
and catalysts for emission control devices; one European

group of business consultants estimates that the U.S. market for air bags, electronic antiskid devices, and emission control devices will be worth over $5 billion a year by 1980.

Safety-related auto improvement is potentially a new opportunity for auto marketing, and a promising new venture for the auto companies. Yet such change remains fixed, necessarily, to the existing automobile market, with its grave and worsening problems of saturation, overelaboration, consumer disillusionment. The technological implications of safety upgrading are also unpromising. Devices like exhaust catalysts and air bags require advances in research and development, yet these advances will not change basic automobile engineering. Their effect on the technology of auto production could be retrogressive, in that air bags and emission control devices are further gadgets to be added on to already complex automobiles. The automation of auto assembling requires a simplification of product design; new auto improvements, like earlier radios or cigar lighters or vinyl roofs, may need to be fixed onto cars by extra assembly workers, working extra "manminutes" at a final assembly line. Safe and clean auto parts are not necessarily convenient to manufacture. Manufacturers may prefer to develop those innovations that improve both the product and the productive process— the Wankel engine, for example, is potentially clean, and, according to GM executives, is also so simple that it can be produced economically, with little labor. Yet the likely major effect of "new" auto upgrading will be to further increase auto dependence on a Fordist organization of mass production.

The auto safety market could offer more remote but

perhaps more encouraging possibilities. Federal regulations, controlling 10 million or more new cars each year, will require an enormous force of inspectors and mechanics, to diagnose and correct automotive defects. (There are already nearly twice as many auto mechanics in the United States as there are doctors and dentists and "related practitioners"; these mechanics will be supported by more and more billions of dollars' worth of capital equipment for diagnosis and for processing information received. Volkswagen's importers already plan a national system for monitoring Volkswagen service, by which hundreds of dealers can plug in their repair shops to a central computer.) Markets for auto diagnostic equipment could provide enticing opportunities in many of the most modish areas of American technology—in the automation of services, government procedures, technical analysis, and in information retrieval services. Auto corporations could produce the equipment and services required by appealingly modern processes, using much capital and technical labor, and no unskilled work. But such a scenario, in which GM or Ford profits by clearing up the debris of the automotive past, would still entail dependence on the traditional auto market; the attractions of diagnostic automation may in any case be denied to U.S. auto corporations by antitrust laws, and by the complexities of the dealer-factory relationship.

Ventures outside the auto safety market may seem more encouraging to the auto companies. The most likely prospects will involve recreational vehicles, mass transportation, and new, simple city cars. Each of these markets, as will be seen, has advantages and disadvantages, both in selling and in production. Prospects outside the transportation business seem relatively unimportant, or remote, and GM's "nonautomotive" operations, which have produced, for example, refrigerators, bomber engines, and M16A1 rifles, account for less than 10 percent of the corporation's sales. (Some of the auto companies' nonautomotive ventures recall the most familiar characteristics of the automobile market. GM produced parts for Apollo Lunar Vehicles—the cars whose malfunctioning drive components turned early astronauts into irate lunar consumers. GM was the main contractor for the MBT-70, or Main Battle Tank, a "European" rather than "Asian-style" tank, which took nine years to develop and was abandoned after being described by the House Appropriations Subcommittee as "unnecessarily complex, excessively sophisticated, and too expensive." According to the *Wall Street Journal*, "a major flaw in the MBT-70 program was that too much emphasis was placed on building a 'dream tank' and too little on cost, Pentagon planners concede": Congress objected to the "automatic weapons loader that some lawmakers feared would break down in combat and require highly skilled technicians to repair." When the project was dropped, Army planners looked for a newer and simpler European tank. They considered three corporations as contractors, GM, Chrysler, and Ford, an eager helper "which a few years [before] submitted to the Pentagon an unsolicited proposal for a tank.")

Recreational Vehicles

The only euphoric transportation executives are managers selling recreational vehicles, or RV's: 700,000 people buy

RV's each year—motor homes, campers, trailers, and other more or less mobile structures. About 4 percent of American families own such vehicles, and further expansion is anticipated; as *Automotive News* puts it, "Torrid Growth Predicted for RV's." Mobile home and RV shares have been among the most favored of Wall Street stocks, and a motor-home stock, Winnebago Industries, was in 1971 the biggest percentage gainer on the New York Stock Exchange. The auto corporations are active in these boom markets both directly and indirectly. They provide trucks and chassis for conversion by independent RV firms: two California motor-home companies opened factories in Warren, Ohio, in order to be near the trucks produced at GM's new Lordstown truck plant. Auto executives are recruited by RV firms, and one Michigan motor-home company, headed by a former president of Ford, employs five former GM executives, including a former chief engineer of the Vega project. GM itself entered the motor-home business in 1973, offering a medium-price motor home, available in many different colors and sizes, with fifteen different "floor plans" for the "living area."

Motor homes express the purest ideal of Sloanist selling. They promise upgrading beyond Sloan's wildest hopes—vehicles equipped with radios, air conditioners, interior trimmings, but also with beds, televisions, vacuum cleaners, deep freezers. They fulfill the vision of GM's first stylist, Harley Earl, who wrote that "you can design a car so that every time you get in it, it's a relief—you have a little vacation," and approach even the convenience of the camper in Tati's film *Traffic*, whose radiator grille could snap up into a barbecue grid. The selling of RV's uses the

techniques and the language, the trade-ups and options and
trade-ins, of the auto market: a Michigan RV dealer told
Automotive News that "saturation" seemed remote, "It
just keeps going. People are always upgrading."

For some corporate philosophers, vacation vehicles represent the direct line of automotive inheritance. The RV
boom is thought to show that leisure can be motorized, in
spite of the decline of the large family car. Vacation travel
inspires the same speculation about the future of the consuming family that adorned discussion of the second and
third family car.* When Chevrolet sponsored an RV festival in Arizona, executives said that the RV boom was the
result of such factors as increased leisure, the 4-day work
week, Monday holidays, park improvements, "the interest
in ecology"; one executive anticipated an orderly upgrading of cars and RV's, via something called a Chevrolet
"Trip Vehicle," which, with a television and "snack
cooker," "offers more for the [traveling family] than a
conventional car but less in the way of facilities (and
expense) than an RV."

RV's offer many advantages of automotive modernity,

---

* Open Road Industries told *Automotive News* that "since it is the
woman who takes primary interest in preserving family togetherness," its
campers appeal to women. Winnebago said, "The motor home is the
ultimate and we are improving on it with such features as built-in
vacuum cleaners, separate freezer compartment, bathtub, etc. Women
appreciate the family being able to travel together with the use of the
facilities while traveling. . . . Salesmen should show [the woman] the
kitchen, bath, closets, and talk to her about keeping house in an RV."
J. Z. DeLorean, GM's prophet of Vega psychology, has said that
Chevrolet's advertising theme, of "Building a Better Way to See the
U.S.A.," should reach the female (or recreational) psyche, because it
pictures entire families in compatible units.

such as their relation to the "interest in ecology." Industry publicity features vistas of natural beauty, in national parks and mountain retreats. The vehicles have names like "Wanderer," "Discoverer," "Utopia," and one company claims to offer "portable environment." GM pursued a theme of environmentalism throughout the development of its motor home—the vehicles are available in four different variations of interior trim, and the name of the trim is noted on the outside of the motor home, "Glacier (blue-green)," "Painted Desert (orange-rust)," "Sequoia (green)," or "Canyon Lands (brown-beige)." Yet the popularity of RV's is also assumed to indicate a continuing national affection for the highway, a reassuring compatibility of modern consciousness and the auto-industrial system. An advertisement addressed to Ford dealers expresses this optimism, pronouncing that "He can't have fun without wheels to get there," that people "have more leisure time than ever. And they're spending that time on the road."

Campers, trailers, and motor homes seem certain to flourish and multiply in the next decades. They re-create some of the true benefits of early automobiles, allowing mobility, solitude, equality of tourism. Unlike most automobiles, vacation vehicles are used for pleasure, and not for the frustrating necessities of traveling to work or to the supermarket. Vacation travel is even relatively economical, in that the average occupancy of automobiles is 1.4 people on drives to and from work, and 3.3 people on vacation trips. Yet recreational vehicles are likely to suffer from general consumer discontent with the waste and hyperbole of automobiles. RV's are already criticized bitterly by

Ralph Nader's associates as unsafe and unreliable, particularly in suspension parts, and GM customers are assured, alarmingly, that their motor homes can be repaired in an "emergency-service program." Campgrounds are crowded, even on the West Coast, where one third of all RV's are bought, and where hundreds of new campsites are built each year; conservationist groups argue that RV's should be banned from national parks, and from many unspoiled districts.

For the auto companies, RV sales offer an easy mode of market expansion, an easy continuation of past policies. But automotive policies may prove as unpopular in vacation selling as in the selling of conventional cars. RV sales will be worth only a small fraction of automobile value, and a fraction to be divided among many different companies. Hundreds of large and small companies compete in the RV market, and these newer companies could be more adventurous than the auto corporations in selling RV's by non-Sloanist techniques; some RV manufacturers complain already about the damaging, high-pressure influence of auto companies and auto dealers. From the perspective of technological change, RV's seem conventional in much the same way that safer and cleaner family cars do. Motor homes and campers, which are lavishly upgraded vehicles, trucks decked with refrigerators, require elaborate assembly techniques, and some RV's are manufactured in converted auto factories. RV's could be built more or less by hand, although at probably reduced "cost efficiency," and GM itself attempted, briefly, some methods of group or team production at the small truck plant where it builds its new motor home; yet any major reorganization by the auto corporations of mass-production work is only a little more likely in motor-home manufacturing than it is in the manufacture of automobiles.

Mass Transportation

The auto corporations may soon consider new ventures in selling mass transportation, in building and planning trolley lines or computerized bus systems. In June 1972, the auto companies participated in a government-sponsored exposition of different kinds of transport, called Transpo '72. GM showed Cadillacs, Vegas, earthmovers, buses, experimental mini-cars, plans for reorganizing the bus system of Rochester, New York; a company representative explained that GM's "objectives for Transpo '72 are to demonstrate that GM is a total transportation organization . . . [a] producer of hardware that will meet the needs of any federal, state, or local transportation system that is planned." Ford displayed a system of trolley cars built under government contract, and Henry Ford pronounced that "entirely new public-transportation concepts" were "urgently" needed, and should be financed in part out of Highway Trust Fund revenues: he said, "Today I am making the formal announcement that Ford is entering the public-transit-system business."

The public-transport business holds the promise of a future federal bonanza, where every city will demand its transportation project. Many of the most expansionist of U.S. corporations participated in mass-transit demonstrations at Transpo, and diversifying aerospace companies were particularly prominent; transit systems were proposed for airports, shopping malls, universities, and eventually for smaller or larger American cities. Corporations could be given contracts to plan and build the public-transport system for a specific city: such contracts would require the enticing modern technologies of computer program design, and of service automation. The cars and trolleys used in such projects would be produced by technically advanced methods, and Cole of GM has said that his corporation could build basic transport "modules," "virtually on-the-shelf" hardware, which would be easy to assemble and store, and could be used variously as containerized freight cars, double-deck trains, transit-stop waiting rooms, covers for moving sidewalks, overstreet passageways.

The auto companies emphasize their concern about the future of urban transport, and a recent GM Annual Report promises "substantial expansion of the GM Research Laboratories, particularly in the areas of transportation and urban planning." Yet most of their projects seem remote from practical application. A few months after the Transpo Exposition, and by arrangement with GM's public relations department, I visited Mr. Spreitzer, the director of the GM transportation planning department, in his office at the GM Technical Center. Spreitzer said that his group of twenty-eight planners, systems analysts, economists, and behavioral scientists was the largest group of its sort in the country, but that it was concerned with "objective analysis, not problem-solving." Ford's group, he said, was smaller, and took a shorter-term view. He said that his group was looking fifteen or twenty-five years into the future, and that he considered it "possible but not probable" that GM would be a public-transportation contractor sometime after 1985. (One of the group's present projects is to compile social and statistical information about all American cities of more than 50,000 inhabitants, and Spreitzer said that the GM data bank was the "largest collection of information [about American cities] anywhere.") The group's relation to GM's productive operations seemed distant; when I asked Mr. Spreitzer about the GM Coach and Bus Division, which invented the GM module system, he recalled the 1965 (antitrust) Consent Decree concerning bus manufacturing, and repeated that "we are an analytic, research group."

It seems scarcely surprising that the auto corporations' transit planning should be less than vigorous—as Spreitzer put it, "the auto, it would appear, is our major product." Yet many of the transport projects proposed at Transpo would support rather than supplant the automobile: at entertainment centers and shopping malls, for example, trolleys would move people to and from peripheral parking lots; and even some systems serving suburban commuters could be substitutes for the use rather than the ownership of cars, as commuters will still depend on cars at night, or on weekends. The sale of mass-transit services is among the less likely of auto-industrial possibilities, and it is affected by the same forces of competitive adjustment and strategic inertia that apply to other such possibilities.

The White House Office of Emergency Preparedness, in its 1972 study of energy conservation (which identified automotive transportation as a major way in which national fuel resources are wasted), describes short-, medium-, and long-term measures for saving energy. In each time period, it cites improvements in mass transport as a valuable and economical proposal: the study's sequence of measures provides a most convincing scenario of likely automotive attitudes to mass-transport systems that might challenge auto sales. In the short term, until 1975, the study argues that improvements in mass-transit and intercity rail-freight services would be valuable, but might have a "possible detrimental effect on the automobile and related industries," and might meet "possible strong resistance from highway and travel lobby groups." In the medium term, until 1980, such measures, together with measures to encourage the sale of small urban cars, would provide great benefits, but might cause a "possible loss in sales to the U.S. auto industry," and "may require increased government involvement." In the long term, past 1980, the situation changes abruptly. New and desirable mass-transit systems would be implemented by Research and Development work: the study argues that by the 1980s "the position of the U.S. transportation industries in the world market place may well depend on investment in [such] R and D." This triple scenario summarizes the auto industry's predicament over mass transit—where present and near-term concern to preserve existing, wasteful auto institutions contradicts the counsels of long-term self-interest.

City Cars

The most promising, for the auto corporations, of all likely automotive ventures involves selling small and simple urban cars. Ventures in selling recreational vehicles and new auto options would use familiar principles of auto marketing; the manufacture of small city cars, by contrast, will bring new developments in auto mass production, and, perhaps, in auto distribution. As seen earlier, a major objective of auto production engineers—often frustrated in the elaboration of the modern market—is to simplify car design. These engineers hope to reduce costs in parts-stamping and final-assembly operations, which remain the most troublesome phases of auto production. Vega designers boast of reducing the number of parts required to make a car, and plastics executives look forward to the days of the basic car body molded out of three fiberglass components: the manufacture of city cars could make possible the further automation of auto-making, subordinated since the 1920s to the upgrading of auto sales.

The U.S. auto corporations have produced experimental versions of urban cars, the size of Honda cars or of small Fiats. GM displays a "hybrid" car which can use either an electric motor or a gasoline engine, and has lent its corporate vehicle proving grounds to an "Urban Vehicle Design Contest." The "concepts manager" of Ford's car research suggests that the use of urban cars, which would serve as "small security vaults" against the criminal elements of cities, could improve the efficiency of urban transportation. The manufacture and use of such cars would have evident advantages for productive efficiency, for the urban environment, for energy conservation. The new cars would produce less pollution and use less fuel than cars with larger engines. Present Hondas are about half as long and little more than half as wide as standard Chevrolets: more Hondas than Chevrolets can be packed into the streets and parking lots of cities.

The use of cheap city cars is a most rational way to improve urban transportation in the short term. Yet for the auto corporations such a development could bring conflict and confusion. The simplification of cars contradicts the history of automotive marketing, the cumulative upgrading which finds its modern expression in option selling or in the recreational vehicle market. The new simple cars might be bought as substitutes for familiar, more expensive compact or subcompact cars: in these circumstances, a decision to offer large numbers of very cheap cars would require the sort of management somersault not yet found in the automobile industry, or in many other profit-maximizing businesses. For the auto companies, the most favorable situation for the introduction of such cars would require government intervention. If all other automobiles were barred or discouraged from entering the centers of certain cities, urban cars could be segregated physically and psychologically from conventional, upgraded automobiles. They would be bought in addition to first, second, and third cars; their publicized appeal would be quite distinct from the attractions of powerful, ferocious, luxurious family cars (and auto advertisements would need to be read according to a rigorous double standard). Yet such a system could not fail to intensify the disillusionment of auto buyers. It would demand an improbable suspension of incredulity on the part of auto consumers—and an even less probable suspension of immediate self-interest by the auto corporations.

Strategies for using small and simple cars—as city cars,

or as taxis, or as rental cars—could solve very many of the
problems of the present auto-industrial system but would
also attack the bases of automotive power. The scenario
for such a solution shows clearly how auto troubles react
upon one another, in production and use and distribution,
and how any radical change will affect simultaneously all
the different structures of automotive support.

City cars could be used economically—and almost immediately—in an urban rental scheme. (Such a scheme has
been tried in French and Dutch projects, where participants
subscribe periodically to an auto rental service. A firm called
Mini-Cars Inc., of Santa Barbara, has produced experimental versions of urban cars: according to *Motor Trend*, the
firm is directed by a former head of GM's Commercial Projects Research Department, with two other former GM
researchers, one of whom "directed research on advanced
power systems," the other having "designed everything from
lunar rovers to high-speed military vehicles." Mini-Cars,
with Budget Rent-A-Car in Los Angeles, now plans to try a
"Select-A-Car" system, where rental cars can be activated
by credit cards, at different urban depots.)

In a rental project, cars could be hired from rental stations throughout a city, perhaps in every parking lot. They
would be used, and left at another station; rental stations,
like parking lots in contemporary cities, could be operated
within walking distance of any office or factory or store.
The cars could be used all day by a succession of renters.
They could be designed with small engines, to carry two
people: even in existing, huge-engined cars, no urban
motorist expects to maintain a high average speed, and on
a normal day in downtown New York, travels at an average

speed of 7 mph. Larger cars could be available, for people with many packages; large and small (but slow and non-polluting) rental trucks would be used for delivering freight in central cities; the rental vehicles would complement mass-transportation projects.

A rental system which barred all but rental vehicles from some areas of cities would need fiscal and political support —but such support is not inconceivable in the context of escalating government concern about the waste and filth of urban transport. (Auto transport is most notoriously inefficient in central cities, and the Office of Emergency Preparedness study of energy conservation concludes that "urban transportation is the prime candidate for action" in saving transport fuel demand: 55 percent of all energy consumed by automobiles is consumed within cities, and more than half of all urban auto trips are of less than ten miles, with an average of 1.4 people in every car.) An efficient system would need to be comprehensive and segregated, and could be attempted first in a restricted area of a central city. It would have advantages in every area of urban transport problems. It would cost a small fraction of the price of new urban mass-transit or people-mover programs, and could be used eventually to support such projects. It would improve traffic safety, as small, low-speed cars would not travel on the same highways as supercharged sedans. It would be economical in saving fuel, increasing the utilization of cars, and avoiding the present situation in which tens of millions of expensive automobiles sit parked in suburban streets from seven at night until eight in the morning, and in city parking lots from nine in the morning until six at night.

The system would reduce pollution because it would use little fuel to move many people: it would also provide a convenient way to introduce new power sources. Electric cars, which are now suitable for fairly short trips, at fairly slow speeds, could be recharged at each parking-lot rental station. Newer suggestions, such as the proposal to use hydrogen as an auto fuel, would be practical only where auto maintenance and service were handled centrally, for an entire fleet. (Such proposals would save gasoline and reduce pollution and noise pollution in central cities by transferring pollution and energy demand to electricity-generating plants—but by using small cars efficiently, a city car rental system would also save energy absolutely.)

A comprehensive network of rental car stations could be used by city governments as a flexible way of controlling traffic. If a government wished to use price incentives to reduce congestion it could impose a higher tax on auto rentals when traffic was heavy. Changing rates could be posted at all rental stations, and motorists in New York City might pay ten dollars a mile to rent a car at Madison Avenue and 48th Street at five o'clock on a Friday afternoon, and fifty cents a mile on Tenth Avenue or on Madison at eleven o'clock that same night. The rental system could raise serious questions of social justice—but city authorities, who would need to support the system politically and perhaps financially, could in theory use the rental cars in as just or as unjust a way as they pleased. Price rationing of congestion discriminates in favor of the rich; a comprehensive system comparable to Mini-Cars' credit-card–activated "Select-A-Car" would leave urban auto transportation at the mercy of the discriminatory, "creditworthy" system of institutional lending. Yet cities, regulating in the first instance a small downtown area, could attempt more ingenious ways of leasing cars, and could offer favorable rates to any group it chose. The system could be as democratic as desired: present, democratic arrangements, where many people can afford cars, and can drive them wherever they like, could persist outside the most congested areas of cities.

Possible rental car systems would have advantages for users, beyond the general and social benefits of saving resources and reducing pollution, and beyond even the greatly increased convenience of city travel. Users would be saved from the frustration and worry of owning a car in a large city. They would save in parking costs, insurance, service, and maintenance. Many auto trips in cities are for the most routine purposes, of commuting to work, or visiting stores and government offices: drivers would lose few advantages of automotive freedom by using small cars for such basic transportation. Users would also save money as the total demand or need for automobiles was reduced. The new cars might sell to rental authorities for as little as $1,000, and their operating costs would be adjusted for the economies of fleet maintenance, and of intensive utilization.* People might use rental cars instead of owning second or first cars, and savings on auto interest and depreciation

---

* Even if small city cars cost almost as much as Vegas to manufacture, they might be sold directly to rental authorities for $1,000, without the expense of elaborate selling, distribution, and advertising. Mini-Cars Inc.'s experimental urban cars should cost $2,500 each, if 25,000 vehicles were produced—but these cars use nonsegregated highways, and have a top speed of 95 mph.

would free large proportions of their income to spend on goods and services other than basic auto transportation.

To the extent that they would use existing streets and parking lots, and would preserve existing principles of individual transportation, rental schemes would be a most moderate way of improving city transport (although they could be used with projects to improve bus and rail services, to introduce new forms of mass transit, even to reduce the total demand for transportation). Yet such arrangements, were they to become widespread, would have the most disruptive consequences for the auto business. The conflict auto companies face in selling small cars would be intensified. The new cars would certainly require fewer options, and fewer model changes, and would be sold without the elaborate appeal of past auto advertising. The idea that cars should be economical instruments for basic transportation would contradict the assumptions of all auto selling. Annual auto sales, and the value of sales, would contract as the utilization of cars increased: consumer spending, and production jobs, would move to other industries. Drivers could choose what sort of vehicle they would use for nonbasic travel outside cities—some might buy upgraded family cars or recreational vehicles, while others could decide to rent larger or smaller cars, for all uses.

Waste has been part of automotive history for the last forty years, yet the waste and worry of urban auto travel now seems a most unsatisfactory instance of national profligacy. The attempt to regulate urban traffic, perhaps by the use of small rental cars, would damage the political coalitions of auto support, as it would damage the basis of automotive selling. A large private rental scheme might offer a bonanza for auto rental companies, for credit-card and parking-lot and auto-service corporations, perhaps for firms manufacturing electric and other new engines, and for computer corporations which would provide the information services required to operate the rental scheme. The interests of auto dealers, auto insurers, energy corporations, would no longer coincide necessarily with auto manufacturers' interests. Rental companies may themselves consider the production of small cars for urban leasing; gasoline and battery and aerospace and other corporations already support research on electric and other unconventional small-car engines; the plastics corporations which perform development work on auto components could consider producing entire bodies for urban vehicles. Auto companies, with their continuing financial and managerial involvement in the conventional auto market, might at worst find themselves producing uncompetitive simplified Vegas, in the adjustments of industrial evolution. Different companies, with a greater or lesser investment in past automotive practice, could face harsh conflict over capital and resources; in such a fragmentation of the auto-industrial complex, it is unlikely that the four U.S. auto corporations would emerge stronger, or more adventurous.

8

Foreign Adventures

The last best hope of automotive expansion leads corporations to more and more distant countries, to Germany and Japan, and to Spain, Brazil, and Indonesia. Yet such foreign adventures will only duplicate for the U.S. auto corporations the dislocation and contention of domestic adjustments. Industrial evolution, in its international form, sets business against business, technology against technology— and nation against nation, as countries and regions struggle over the world balance of wealth and productivity, of auto development, mass production, worker alienation, industrial waste, automotive civilization.

International adjustments seem challengingly attractive to U.S. auto corporations. Like their counterparts in late-Victorian railroad or textile industries, modern auto executives sound most vigorous and optimistic when describing foreign expansion. The coming reorganization of international auto production inspires executives to perceptions of "tremendous potential," "tremendous challenge," "virtually unlimited market(s)," unknown in the U.S. auto business since the 1920s and 1930s. Yet such a reorganization will bring conflict far beyond the troubles of Toyota and Volkswagen imports into the United States. It could bring struggles at least as bitter as those faced by British industries, or by auto companies in their projects for making city cars and other "high-technology" products: struggles which go beyond even the competition of international auto companies to the joint Japanese/European/U.S. endeavor of imposing the "American plan" of auto-industrial development on ever more industries, in ever less developed countries.

All senior auto executives speculate publicly about the future of the world auto market. A representative account of U.S. auto ambitions is provided by E. M. Estes, one of GM's rising leaders, and a former vice-president in charge of overseas operations. He predicts much faster automotive growth abroad than in the United States, and has said that the foreign market offers a "tremendous challenge" to GM. In the next few years, he expects the greatest potential for growth in "Southern Europe and South America. I would say South America for sure, if it weren't for political problems." Argentina seems promising, and he considers that "Brazil is the high spot." Eastern European ventures offer exciting hopes; the major potential for growth in Western Europe will come from such optional equipment as automatic transmissions and air conditioners, and Estes, looking forward to multinational upgrading, notes that in 1970 only 9 percent of GM's German Opels had automatic transmissions, only 5 percent vinyl tops, and only 2 percent power steering. GM executives also expect automotive growth outside Europe and South America; the 1972 GM Annual Report describes the company's activities in Japan, Malaysia, Zaire, South Korea, and the Philippines, and proclaims that "strong growth rates for motor vehicle sales are anticipated during the next several years in the developing countries of Africa and Southeast Asia."

International auto markets seem to promise all the expansive attractions that U.S. corporations no longer expect from the domestic auto business. American companies are well placed to participate in world auto growth, having established many of their foreign operations in the 1920s, when around 80 percent of all automobiles were made in the United States. They express their international enthusiasm in present plans for capital expansion. Both GM and Ford emphasize foreign investment in their 1973 budgets, with Ford active in Spain and Asia, and GM planning expansion for Opel in Germany, Belgium, Denmark, and Switzerland; since 1960, GM's foreign vehicle production has doubled, while its U.S. production increased by around one half, and its production in Latin America and South Africa increased almost nine times over. Corporate ventures are likely to attempt all the permutations of multinational production, making cars and car components abroad for sale in the United States (as in the recent troubles with Toyotas, Pintos, and other small cars), cars in Europe for sale in Europe, cars in developing countries for sale in other developing countries, cars and car components in developing countries for sale in Europe and Japan: Joseph Godfrey of the GM Assembly Division, who believes that increasing domestic productivity is the answer to automotive troubles, describes such ventures as a "trend," saying, "I don't think we should make our cars overseas. This is more serious than most people think. This is the trend, and it's what's wrong with this country."

Certain foreign auto manufacturers and foreign auto industries appear to enjoy the self-sustaining momentum that the U.S. companies experienced in the 1920s—the momentum of British railroads in the 1850s, or of certain modern American computer-based industries. In the adjustments of international automotive business—market expansion, economic growth, technological advance—social and business popularity now favors countries outside North America (although in the 1970s, unlike the 1920s, corporations from different countries can share the benefits of such momentum). Agnelli of Fiat found an "auto boom" in the United States before the Depression, in Western Europe in the 1950s, and in Japan in the 1960s; he hoped for similar booms in the late 1970s and 1980s in Southern and Eastern Europe, Africa, Asia. To envious U.S. auto executives, such a pattern of world growth seems bleakly probable. The Japanese industry, with its most recent boom, is acknowledged to be a major competitor in the crisis of international productivity; as seen earlier in the troubled history of Toyota imports, Japanese competitive successes are the result of economic growth and efficiency, rather than of "poor quality" production, or of access to "cheap labor."

In the rise and fall of auto-industrial development, Japanese corporations are now prime survivors. Japanese automotive growth began in the middle 1950s. Ford and GM had dominated the early Japanese auto market. By 1929 their local assembly plants supplied 85 percent of domestic sales. In the late 1930s, when Japanese production became concentrated on trucks, buses, and military vehicles, the U.S. companies were expelled; during the Second World War, Toyota, Nissan (which makes Datsuns), and Isuzu Motors (which is now owned in part by GM) became major war contractors. Like many other Japanese industries, the auto business began its postwar recovery with U.S. military procurement during the Korean War. In 1952, Japan made 100,000 motor vehicles, of which most were army trucks and only 5,000 were passenger cars; by 1962, passenger-car production had increased fifty times over, and by 1972 another fifteen times.

Such growth surpassed even the successes of Henry Ford's Model T. Like the early U.S. industry, the Japanese auto business enjoyed a simultaneous expansion of production, productivity, capital investment, technological proficiency. Throughout the 1960s, Japanese firms built newer, bigger, and better auto factories, spending large proportions of their incomes on new capital equipment. Japanese companies are at least as secretive about the productivity of their operations as GM or Ford; but a British government study estimates that output per manhour in the Japanese auto business at least doubled in the 1960s, while the domestic price of small Japanese cars fell at least as fast as the price of Model T's in the 1920s. During its rapid expansion, the Japanese auto business bought technical knowledge from U.S. and European firms: before its association with Isuzu, GM had technical agreements with at least five Japanese components firms, and about sixty U.S. auto components firms enjoyed similar arrangements. Yet Japanese auto firms also developed an indigenous auto technology, and a U.S. Department of Commerce guide to Japan now writes that the corporations "emerged from the technological dependence on western producers by designing exemplary assembly plants and competitive automobiles."

Japanese auto mass production is in many ways more advanced than modern U.S. production. Factories are newer, and more expensive; where U.S. auto technology now seems demoralized and defensive, Japanese research into auto production has been among the most expansionary sectors of national technical development. The guiding Industrial Structure Council of the Ministry for International Trade has designated "industries that rely heavily on assembly lines" as an area where Japanese business should concentrate, and Japan now leads the world in the refinement of Fordist production. A British Toyota dealer, asked on British television why Toyota shipped complete export cars halfway around the world, said scornfully that his parent company would not consider assembling cars in Europe, because of the great sophistication and "tremendous computerization" of Japan's domestic assembly procedures. Toyota's home factory in Nagoya is said to be among the most automated in the world, and uses many-talented robots, known as "magic hands," which are at least as advanced as the Lordstown Unimates, and manipulate several different machines successively. Nissan uses actual Unimates, specially adapted in Japan, and is eager to hire scientists from the U.S. space program. In accordance with the guide-lines of the Industrial Structure Council, Japanese corporations produce exemplary machinery for automated mass production: U.S. manufacturers buy Japanese robots for use in particularly dangerous stamping operations, and one Japanese capital-goods firm recently sold automated presses, which ingest metal and disgorge truck doors, to Ford of Argentina and to GM in Germany.

Toyota City in Nagoya is the capital, the Ford River Rouge, of the modern automobile business. Japanese proficiency goes beyond assembly technology to the design of new automobiles, and new ways of organizing work. Japanese cars no longer seem comical to Americans, as they did in 1959, when Nissan's IJ.S. subsidiary sold exactly three Datsun Cedrics (named after Little Lord Fauntleroy). Toyo Kogyo, which makes Mazdas, was the first auto corporation to develop and mass-produce reliable Wankel engines; Toyota and Nissan experiment with city cars, clean cars, electric cars, recreational cars, and other vehicles essential to automotive modernity. Japanese corporations also attempt new techniques for arranging repetitive work. Toyo Kogyo's Hiroshima factory alters and breaks up assembly-line rhythms, and Nissan uses the "quality control circle" methods noted by GM's personnel executives, where seven or eight workers form a group to help increase company productivity. In almost every area of Fordist improvement, Japanese industry is a cynosure of world admiration. When I first visited Lordstown, in 1970, Japanese auto factories were considered interesting only as the source of imported Toyotas. In 1972, a woman worker at Lordstown told me, categorically, that "foreign people have better working conditions than we do. . . . We have higher wages, but also a higher cost of living. The Japanese have guaranteed jobs for life, and low-cost housing loans and, in Japan, auto workers on the night shift get paid extra for losing their 'life at home.' " Another Lordstown worker also described the Japanese ideal, in testimony to the Kennedy Subcommittee Hearings on Worker Alienation: in Japan, auto workers "have recreation areas during their breaks. They can either play ping-pong or they can swim. . . . If you want to take a look at some things, we are the Number One country in the world today as far as power and life and living standards and everything, take a look at Japan's working conditions."

In their foreign projects, and notably in their joint ventures with Japanese manufacturers, the U.S. auto corporations aspire to share the evident benefits of international automotive growth. Yet the pace and ease of growth is far from uniform in different foreign countries. Some European companies face much the same troubles as the U.S. auto business, with consumer disillusionment, market congestion, depressed productivity, demoralized auto technology, with auto workers at least as discontented as workers in America. Even Japan expects slower automotive growth, and comparable problems of automotive marketing. The argument of this book has been that American auto troubles are caused by the development of forces within and around the mass-production auto business: similar forces can be expected to develop with the similar "auto booms" of other countries. All growing auto industries require a deformation of national resources in favor of auto transportation, and all use a monotonous and repressive technology of mass production. The U.S. auto business took forty years to grow from youthful euphoria to its present distress—yet just as the booms of foreign industries were achieved relatively fast, so also their troubles may now become accelerated, in the world interrelationships of technology, natural resources, and consumer discontent.

In simple saturation, of people to automobiles, the United States still leads all other car-producing countries. Yet market saturation, as shown in the recent troubles of American auto selling, has to do also with congestion, social convenience, consumer expectations. The United States, for example, is relatively uncongested in the ratio of land to automobiles, and of paved roads to automobiles.* Such comparisons are reflected in the pleasure, and safety, of auto use. The Japanese government now expects little increase in domestic auto sales; Japan's traffic problems are so well known that Northwest Orient Airlines advertises that one of its flights from New York to Tokyo, halfway around the world, arrives in Japan "well after the Tokyo rush-hour traffic." Problems of auto safety, urban pollution, traffic frustration, are as oppressive in Tokyo or Cologne as they are in American cities.

International auto companies now propose, in their French, German, or Japanese markets, the sort of option-loaded selling developed in the United States in the 1930s and 1950s. Estes of GM looked forward to vistas of air conditioners and vinyl tops installed on German Opel cars; Umberto Agnelli of Fiat says that in France and Germany

---

* A recent World Bank "Working Paper" on Transportation found that the United States had five motor vehicles registered for every ten people, compared to 2.1 per ten people in Germany, and 1.2 per ten people in Japan, yet the United States had only 11 vehicles per square kilometer of national land, compared to 52 vehicles in Germany, and 34 in Japan, and only 39 per kilometer of paved road, compared to 44 in Germany and 96 in Japan.

"the point of [auto] saturation has already been reached," and that most future growth in the Western European auto market will be in the "over 1.5 liter car class." *The Economist* of London anticipates an increased desire for "fun motoring" on the part of European two-car families, and like Agnelli, Japanese manufacturers expect on orderly trading up in power and luxuriousness by domestic auto consumers. Yet such a future seems ever less likely. Many automotive problems, including troubles of environmental protection and energy conservation, are common to all advanced countries: a national upgrading towards larger and faster cars will appear radically undesirable in the context of a crisis of Western European petroleum supplies, or of a crisis of pollution in downtown Tokyo. There is a world market in consumer products and even, perhaps, in consumer attitudes; the new offerings, and the public and private goods and services which distract Americans from spending more on further automotive upgrading, are available today or tomorrow to European and Japanese consumers. (One indication of the "maturity," or decadence, of European marketing is shown in recent trivial disputations between American and European auto designers. According to *Automotive News*, GM's head stylist, William Mitchell, has attacked Italian auto stylists as "exhibitionists," saying that one well-known auto prototype "is no longer an automobile. Its interior looks like Dracula's bathtub." He also lunges at Mercedes, asking if its styling department is "still alive," and saying of the Mercedes SL sports coupe that "with this Japanese pagoda roof, the car looks laughable." The chief engineer of Daimler-Benz fought back, and "called Mitchell ultimately responsible for pernicious and dangerous styling, particularly the W front end as on the Pontiac"; he "compared the jutting fenders and pointed nose to hatchets, and called the grille a 'cow-catcher for pedestrians.' ")

European auto executives seem at least as demoralized as their American counterparts, and perceive the same catastrophes. The major spectacles of European motoring have lost their glamour: a recent national Motor Show in London was acclaimed in the local motoring press with an editorial lamenting the "debilitating effect of bad times," and, in the London *Times*, with anticipation of the day when German manufacturers would encounter "the sort of labor problems that have crippled the Italian and British car-makers." Many of the complaints of European manufacturers are depressingly familiar. Fiat executives describe the crisis of auto productivity, and the futility of domestic capital investment. The chairman of Volkswagen complains of an "explosive increase in the cost of labor" which could be only partly counterbalanced by corporate efforts at "intensifying automation and introducing harsh saving measures"; Opel's American chief executive laments the "labor shortages" and "high rate of absenteeism" he finds in Germany. French, German, and Swedish auto corporations are unable to fill their factories with native workers, and employ immigrant labor from Turkey, the Middle East, North and East Africa. In Swedish auto assembly factories only half of all workers are Swedish, and one fifth are women. Some German auto plants employ workers of thirty different nationalities. The Yugoslavian town of Nis, near the Bulgarian border, has a disastrously high accident rate: the reason for it is that every day in the summer vacation period, some

2,000 cars pass through Nis driven by exhausted Turkish workers, racing home from jobs in northern European factories—in, for example, Volkswagen's or Opel's auto plants.

The Japanese auto business, with its new, improved technology, and its new, expanded markets, can expect less disruption than its European or American competitors. Yet even as an international model of automotive modernity, the Japanese industry faces certain of the problems inherent in auto development. The forces that supported the Japanese auto boom could also exacerbate its later troubles. Beyond the market problems caused by auto pollution and congestion, Japanese corporations may face dislocations as their rate of auto growth slows (although not necessarily the labor unrest that U.S. executives so eagerly anticipate, as when an official of Ford's Asian subsidiary pronounces that "there is a new, educated postwar generation coming into influence in Japan's work force. They are not going to work with the same sense of national purpose as before"). The organization of mass assembly work will remain monotonous: companies like Nissan and Toyo Kogyo attempt job-enrichment programs presumably in anticipation of the possibility of worker discontent. The technical limitations of Fordist auto production may also disturb automotive growth. One of the factors that made possible Japan's auto boom was the availability of international auto technology: in the world market for scientific discovery, American, Japanese, and European firms could experience more or less simultaneously changes in the balance of high and low technologies, from assembly production to automated and computer-based manufacturing. The government guide-line designating assembly-line industries as important to Japanese business also called for growth in the production of "high quality" goods, in "technology-intensive" industries, and in information industries: Japanese business, which in the late 1960s may have seemed suited to a mass-production phase of world industrialization, will now compete with the United States in ever more advanced technologies—perhaps at the expense of older and less expansionary businesses, such as the automobile and other assembly industries.*

It is these social and productive troubles of advanced auto economies that inspire auto executives in their hopes for expansion in underdeveloped areas. All international auto corporations share the faith of GM's representatives, in "Southern Europe and South America," in "Africa and

---

* One indication of likely changes in the Japanese economy is given by the situation of Matsushita Electrical, the leading profit-maker of all Japanese corporations. Matsushita's recent development followed closely the evolution of "dynamic" U.S. corporations in a changing national economy. The company's early expansion was based on television and other appliance assembly industries. Yet by 1971 it faced very slow growth and a domestic market where three fifths of all Japanese homes had color television sets, and where women's consumer associations had organized a successful national boycott of expensive home-produced color TV's. According to *Fortune*, Matsushita executives therefore concluded that "the best way to stimulate demand [was] to develop new products, mainly through research in the company's own extensive laboratories." The new products included such classic upgradings as devices to freeze TV images so consumers can "analyze sports events," and to allow "youthful viewers to sing along (electronically) with pop stars." Yet the company—which is meanwhile expanding its foreign production in Singapore, Taiwan, and Puerto Rico, and which uses elaborate job-enrichment programs in its domestic operations—also developed such advanced products, typical of high-technology U.S. business, as components for prefabricated houses, equipment for medical and government services, a computerized system for controlling traffic congestion in Yokohama.

Southeast Asia." Automotive growth, whose advantages sustained the economic expansion of the United States, Western Europe, and Japan, is now expected to release its blessings in ever new nations, where roads are ever emptier, skies ever cleaner, workers ever less restive, customers ever less jaded. Agnelli of Fiat develops his theory of successive auto booms, in such countries as Spain, Poland, Yugoslavia, Argentina, where Fiat is now dominant; the chairman of Volkswagen achieved his present position after a successful tour of duty at VW do Brasil, which controls two thirds of the booming Brazilian auto business, where "absenteeism averages only 2 percent against 14 percent in Germany"; a Minister for Technology in the British government celebrates the Cortina, a car produced by Ford of Britain, and assembled in various factories around the world, with the pronouncement that "the Cortina has endeared itself to people from the United States to Korea, Australia to Angola."

Auto managers seem most openly optimistic in the underdeveloped world. Ford's much publicized recent ventures include building a giant auto factory in Spain, at a cost of around $160 million; the enthusiastic European business press reveals that "General Franco and Mr. Henry Ford II have been personally involved" in planning the project, which displays many of the essential advantages of foreign expansion. Perhaps two thirds of the Spanish Fords will be exported, by agreement with the government, and because few Spanish consumers can afford the compact-sized cars that Ford plans to build. The venture will also achieve the corporate ambition of bringing factories to needy workers, instead of bringing workers to factories, as German auto makers must do when they hire Spanish and other immigrant workers: when Ford was deciding where in Spain it would build its plant, it enjoyed the most lavish national publicity, and, according to the London *Financial Times,* "hundreds of letters pour[ed] into Madrid urging the attractions of different towns ... like that of the girl who begged Ford to come to her town so that her father could return from his work in Germany to live with the family."

(The Eastern European auto market holds more promise for French and Italian corporations than for Ford or General Motors. Fiat dominates foreign auto investment in the area, producing around 300,000 cars a year in the Soviet Union, Poland, and Yugoslavia. Rumania, which often offers free gasoline to tourists, describes itself as a "motorists' paradise"; Renault manufactures 20,000 cars a year in Rumania, and ships Rumanian-made gearboxes and axles to its factories in France. U.S. companies are more likely to sell trucks in Eastern Europe than passenger cars, and the auto market will remain limited by national income and by the willingness of governments to spend capital and national resources on providing highways, parking lots, and gasoline for mass auto use. Agnelli's hope is that by 1980, 10 million automobiles will be registered in Eastern Europe and the Soviet Union—a small fraction of expected registrations in the U.S.)

Spanish or Rumanian projects are only the most immediate and likely of automotive ventures. Beyond South and East Europe, the U.S. companies and their foreign competitors aspire to wider and wider expansion, expecting the sort of welcome that Ford found from General Franco. New expansion proposed in 1972 alone involved GM, Ford,

Volkswagen, and Toyota in the Philippines, GM and Ford in South Korea, GM in Malaysia and Thailand, Volvo in Indonesia, Ford in Taiwan: when the *Wall Street Journal* examined prospects for reconstruction in South Vietnam, it found Japanese companies investigating the ceramic clay of the Mekong Delta, and the "small, particularly succulent Vietnamese banana"—with Ford International searching hopefully for a convenient auto manufacturing facility.

Expansion to underdeveloped countries is the rigorous answer to automotive troubles. It fits the necessities of rational industrial readjustment, of international survival. Orderly business evolution requires a perpetual movement of capital—late-Victorian British businesses invested abroad while Japan and India assaulted the world textile market, and modern "dynamic" U.S. corporations attempt new ventures in higher technologies and more advanced markets. In such a scenario, Japanese or American firms might build cars in East Asia, for sale locally or in home markets. International advantage would be balanced evenly, according to free competition in labor, capital, and natural resources. Local workers would find well-paid jobs in auto factories, and corporations would dispense with expensive projects to automate production and enrich production work (auto plants in underdeveloped countries use much more labor and much less advanced machinery than plants in Europe or Japan—Henry Ford's ideal of auto production standardized in Detroit, São Paolo, and Barcelona has been forgotten, and Volvo's Asian factories are not noted for their job-improvement programs). Underdeveloped countries would not demand strict pollution controls in new factories, and citizens of the United States and Japan need not endure the construction of additional noisy, dirty auto-plants; auto corporations will earn attractive profits for their national shareholders.

Such adjustments are already attempted by various international industries. One U.S. executive has said, looking forward to the multinational production of industrial components, that "In the future, manufacturing is going to be more a matter of professional management of resources worldwide than of operating individual national plants." (The Dana auto-components firm advertises that it is "many different things in many different countries": "Driveshafts in Mexico! Axles in Korea! . . . Gaskets in India! Transmissions in England! Universal Joints in Venezuela!") The resources to be managed will be human and environmental as well as material. Many corporations, such as Matsushita in its Taiwanese and Singapore operations, employ foreign workers to perform monotonous and repetitive jobs: a report on work and immigrant workers by the French National Employers' Confederation laments that "even foreign workers will not take certain jobs except on a strictly temporary basis, while for many jobs it has always been necessary to seek out labor of a less and less developed sort." Even pollution has become a matter for international trade, with environmental purity an increasingly scarce and luxurious resource. By building noxious factories in foreign countries, corporations can help to preserve their own national environments. The economist Milton Friedman has reassured *Fortune* that the United States will import clean air when it buys Japanese steel, because the steel consumed in the United States will be made in factories that pollute the air of Japan, not Indiana. Japan is also concerned with the global balance of industrial waste, and plans foreign expansion of its heavy industries, at coastal sites in Korea, Taiwan, and other neighboring states. To the auto corporations, these refinements of comparative advantage seem a most persuasive model: they help to inspire present automotive fervor in the underdeveloped world.

The trouble with the "foreign" scenario for automotive expansion is that no industry can expect free competition in labor, capital, social and natural development. Human and economic resources do not move around the world like oil in a pipeline. A major shift to foreign production would cause dislocation and unemployment at home: companies cannot hope for the easy adjustments imagined by the *Wall Street Journal* editorial writers who allocated "low-technology, labor-intensive industries" to "less-developed countries," noting that "some [American] workers and executives will find their old skills outdated and will have to learn new ones."

The endeavor to create local consumer markets in underdeveloped countries seems immediately and perhaps also in the long run futile. Even Agnelli, in his discussion of successive auto booms, concedes that "political instability" and "low levels of personal income" may disturb the momentum of auto expansion in "emerging countries." The problem of selling cars to people without bicycles is likely to defy the brightest automotive ingenuity. In Spain, which is one of the most promising of all "new" auto markets, average national income per person per year would go about one third of the way to buying a Chevrolet Impala; in Brazil (GM's "high spot"), workers join together in groups of one hundred or more to buy locally made Volkswagens, and subscribe to car "lotteries." There are more passenger cars registered in Los Angeles County than in the whole of Africa: Engels described British manufacturers' attempts at forcing "the Negroes of the Congo into the civilization attendant upon Manchester calicos"—and in 1971 both GM and Ford started to build new assembly plant facilities in Zaire, the former Belgian Congo, where national income per person is just sufficient to buy a radio for a standard American car. Even beyond such financial limits, a new auto market would require roads, service stations, supplies of petroleum, all the institutions of auto-industrial growth. The development of the Southeast Asian auto business, so "strong" in GM's anticipation, can illustrate some of these difficulties—and also some of the more general troubles of automotive organization.

U.S. auto executives have set about selling cars in Southeast Asia with all the dispatch of Buick salesmen in the late 1930s. A local Ford manager described his hopes for the "fast-growing vehicle market of Southeast Asia": "The Asian-Pacific markets in this vast region contain approximately one billion people—more than one third of the world's population. But they have less than three percent of the world's vehicles. . . ." What scope for growth! Indonesia! Three vehicles for every thousand people! Taiwan! Six per thousand! Ford established new local subsidiaries, and consecrated its ventures with a ceremonial Asian tour by Henry Ford. Corporations invoked the favored traditions of 1938 Sloanism: *Automotive News* reveals that "Ford, as a prelude to a growing commitment in Asia, is backing motor sport in several countries." The U.S. companies behaved with apparent ferocity in these new markets, where

Japanese manufacturers were dominant throughout the 1960s; the *Japan Economic Journal,* claiming that U.S. corporations took advantage of the Japanese embarrassment in Taiwan and South Korea caused by Chinese trading, discovers an Asian "automobile war" between Japan (Toyota and Nissan) and the United States in the form of GM and Ford, as U.S. corporations start "aggressive moves to advance into the Southeast Asian market."

The major Asian efforts of GM and Ford are directed to their new "utility vehicles," or Asian cars. Ford's Fiera and GM's Bedford Harimau were launched in 1972. The Harimau, made in Malaysia, sells for $1,400. The Fiera, which costs around $1,200, has been described by the president of Ford (Asia-Pacific) as "a modern Model T for the masses": "Such a vehicle," he says, "would have a virtually unlimited market." The first Fieras are manufactured in the Philippines: Ford, which is spending around $40 million on expansion in Taiwan, also hopes to equip its multi-Asian cars with cylinder blocks made in Thailand, diesel engines from South Korea, transmissions from Indonesia, electrical components from Singapore. The Fiera was displayed at the 1972 Transpo Exposition in Washington, and, described as "just one step up from the bullock cart or the bicycle," it is color-coordinated and available in six different models.

The investment required for such projects is considerable, even by U.S. standards. In 1972, GM and Ford committed themselves to spending more money on capital expansion in Taiwan, South Korea, and the Philippines alone than GM spent on its entire and vaunted Lordstown project. Yet the market for cars produced with this capital remains mysterious. The Malaysian Harimau sells for more than three times the national per capita income of Malaysia; the Fiera, whose price has increased notably since Ford's early estimates, costs over five times more than the national per capita income in the Philippines. Times do not seem propitious even for wealthier Asian citizens to buy large numbers of automobiles. Problems of congestion and pollution are already serious in the most impoverished Asian cities. Most cars are concentrated in capital cities: three quarters of all Thai automobiles in Bangkok, more than a third of Indonesian cars in Djakarta and of Philippine cars in Manila; the number of cars in South Korea increased two and a half times between 1966 and 1971, and half of the cars are in Seoul. Manila receives more than 2,000 tons of exhaust fumes each day; the *Far East Economic Review* reports that auto pollution, from 200,000 cars, 600,000 registered motorcycles, hundreds of thousands of military vehicles, has killed almost every tree in Saigon (which is "nicknamed 'Hondaville' by the U.S. ambassador"). Seoul is one of the ten most polluted cities in the world, and its level of "pollutant fallout" is 300 percent higher than the level in New York: November 1971 was designated in Seoul as "car-pollution eradication month."

These effects of automotive civilization are only one part of the adjustments needed to sustain a Southeast Asian auto market. Countries will require new, expensive highways, the bias of national transportation which characterized automotive growth in the United States (comparable to the enthusiastic overinvestment in railway transport found in Britain in the mid-nineteenth century). The Philippines, where major road construction is now expected, provides a clear example of this distortion: the country had a foreign-built railroad in the late nineteenth century, which is now obsolete; many of its transport needs can be served most economically by inter-island shipping. The problems of energy supply which preoccupy developed countries will also affect Asian countries. Auto use can only exacerbate such problems, including the problems of South Korea, which in the early 1960s consumed one third of its energy in the form of indigenous coal, and less than 10 percent as imported oil, but which by 1971 used a slightly lower proportion of coal, and almost half its energy in the form of oil. Nations with new, foreign-owned auto industries can anticipate an auto-based pattern of transportation loans, as the U.S.-Japanese "automobile war" affects the policies of foreign aid and international institutional support. The World Bank "Working Paper" on Transportation summarizes this development: "There has been a steady trend away from railways and in favor of highways in the modal distribution of transport lending. Up to 1960, railway lending accounted for more than half of all Bank transport loans and amounted to twice that for highways ... [with] the general worldwide growth of motorization, highway financing became the dominant feature of the Group's transport activities in the 1960s."*

---

* Auto executives sometimes look forward to sales in China. James Roche, the former chairman of GM, said that he was "greatly interested in the Chinese market"; when he visited Japan in 1971, nervous Japanese competitors feared that GM was about to "break into the [Chinese] market of 750 million people through the Tokyo gateway." Toyota executives have toured China, and sold automobiles to a visiting Chinese table-tennis team; some auto corporations show the same optimistic spirit as the Monsanto Chemicals representative who told the *Wall*

also 300 to
Chinese govt.

Corporate worries about the "political instability" of new auto markets can be summarized by asking whether developing countries will accept a pattern of economic growth distorted in favor of motorized transportation. Such countries need investment, and may tolerate the import of foreign pollution—but could also choose to welcome industries that provide more local advantages than the auto business offers. Even GM's and Ford's "utility vehicles," which unlike ordinary passenger cars are not designed for use in capital cities, consume valuable fuel resources, and require some maintenance, with some form of roads or tracks. Auto expansion is for Southeast Asian countries a hundred-year project; and Ford's best planners cannot foresee how the world auto business, or the Ford Motor Company, will look in 2080. Developing countries may be able, in the next few decades, to ask the questions which Americans, with their decades of investment in transportation institutions, with their "inertia of use and wont," can no longer answer—questions about the economic rationality of automotive transport, about the relative advantages of different ways of moving people and things, even about

---

Street Journal that his company had started selling chemicals in China: "You just can't look at a market of that size and not believe that eventually a lot of goods are going to be sold there. One aspirin tablet a day to each of those guys, and that's a lot of aspirin." Yet such aspirations would be inappropriate for the auto business. GM's major Chinese sale involved heavy earth-moving equipment, shipped via an Italian exporter. Prospects for selling light trucks, or automobiles, seem much less promising. Every Chinese province except Tibet now manufactures its own trucks. The Chinese, whose industries use the most rigorous techniques for recycling wastes, effluents, even the silver in liquids left over from solutions used to develop films and X-rays, are hardly prime candidates for the benefits of automotive organization on the "American plan."

the real benefits of transportation itself as a social good. There is no question that the international auto corporations intend a major increase in foreign production. Such a move fits automotive ideas of free trade in world economic development. Yet it is likely also to bring the direst troubles, both at home and abroad. Foreign expansion, involving proposals as expensive as the Lordstown project, might be a substitute for technologically advanced domestic diversification, into city cars, or mass transportation. The American auto corporations require domestic political support, and such support could be damaged if companies imported into the United States large numbers of foreign-made cars: most automotive importing is likely to be achieved in the supply of components, or by independent auto-parts producers. In developed foreign markets, American corporations will find the same problems of selling that they face at home— and, in developing countries, problems with inadequate national wealth, and with the automotive model of economic growth. The expectations of international auto adventurers have, in these situations, little relation to a plausible reality. The troubles of automotive growth remain fixed, still, to a traditional pattern of expansion, as shaped by the inherent contradictions of auto-industrial development.

9
Paradise Lost

All the troubles and hopes and preoccupations of the automobile business lead back to a pattern of industrial inertia —a pattern of obsolescence in selling and production, in expansion, down to most recent strategies for diversification and for foreign growth, in social location. Even beyond economic behavior, and beyond the characteristic caution of aging businesses, the auto industry faces the direst and least tractable problems of social obsolescence. Like all dominant national industries—and like the British railroad industry in the mid-nineteenth century—the auto business depended for its early, glorious growth on the sustenance of social and institutional partiality. Such support provided roads, a favorable tax structure, a dispersal of cities and jobs. It encouraged the decay of alternative modes of transportation, and suspended rational calculations of the costs of auto development and auto waste: it made possible the great and sustained power of American demand for automobiles.

Automotive growth required the technological priority of Fordist mass production, and the opportunities of mass consumption, and also a favoritism of national development. Yet it is exactly this structure of social support that seems most unreliable in present auto troubles, at once the hope and the nemesis of auto development. The recent difficulties of auto selling are caused in part by the collapse of such institutional support, by new public preoccupation with the irrationality and occasional inconvenience of auto use, with the cumulative costs of past auto excesses. At the same time, the apparent inevitability of auto travel in states and cities designed for automobiles is a major force sustaining auto sales and profits—just as the "inertia of use and wont," which Veblen found in British railroad investment and in the planning of nineteenth-century economic and urban development, was responsible for the lingering successes of the demoralized British rail industry. Meanwhile, in yet another conflicting role, this same social inertia of auto development also contributes to the business immobility of auto corporations, which, expecting continued support and continuing, if depressed, profits, are unable to change their habitual strategies.

Consumer preference for automobiles, in the context of social support for auto use, seems more soberly self-interested than mysterious and absolute. Beyond its evident qualities—in offering freedom, independence, privacy, sensations of power—auto transportation has provided the advantages of participation in a most favored sector of the national economy. There seems no need to propose an unexplainable "affinity" between Americans and automobiles: rational consumers would in any case choose to travel on socially subsidized highways, in socially favored cars. Highway construction is only the most tangible part of such subvention. Auto and fuel taxes are used largely to encourage further auto use; the costs of auto use in pollution, destruction of cities, waste of national environmental and energy resources, have been charged, historically, to the general revenue, or to posterity. Where national planning, business incentives, and property taxation favor trucking, it is reasonable to send freight by road rather than on less wasteful railroads. Where all but a tiny percentage of citizens travel to work beyond walking distance, and where public-transit services are decayed or have disappeared, it has been reasonable for 82 percent of Americans to commute to and from work in the automobiles they support as taxpayers. (The psychological appeal of auto transport, in this situation, is itself a consequence of historical partiality. Just as the English felt a joyous mania for nineteenth-century railroads, and as Japanese consumers spent comparatively reckless amounts on television sets and other consumer electrical goods that dominated national economic ascendancy in the 1960s, so, for American consumers, automobiles were the products that corresponded best to a most ecstatic moment of national development.)

Social partiality made possible auto domination and the extraordinary profits of the auto industry. Yet because it was supported by quite specific partiality, auto power is comprehensible, contingent, reversible. It required national sustenance, which will be reduced as auto ascendancy declines. Auto sales and profits were able to expand not only because of the opportune efficiency of auto companies, but also because the costs of auto development were ignored or deferred. The 1940s, 1950s, and 1960s brought a consequent overinvestment in auto transport, whose costs now seem ever more apparent. As with the auto companies' industrial decline relative to newer businesses, so an increased national investment in auto support would amount to throwing good resources after bad. The economic troubles of the auto industry are tied to its social troubles: as the industry's rise changed national life, so its decline will bring dislocations barely imaginable in modern, auto-centered cities.

In the present situation of auto difficulty, social support for increased auto use is already fractured and disintegrated. Commuters still find it cheap to travel by automobile —but such travel may also be inconvenient and frustrating, and may soon be increasingly expensive. The discontent of some consumers, particularly in large cities, where the disadvantages of auto-based planning are first apparent, seems in part a reaction against past extremes of auto enthusiasm. More concretely, modern auto consumers are in fact paying a price, in money and convenience, for the past distortion of national development, for decades of overinvestment in auto institutions. In the next ten or twenty years, the real costs of the present and historical structures of automotive support will become ever more evident—and ever more disruptive of auto expansion.

The waste left by auto development will seem less and less tolerable—a waste which is integral to the ways in which cars are made and sold and used. Auto transportation is already seen as a major social expense by all government agencies concerned with preserving national resources, the natural environment, national energy supplies. The arguments of these agencies—of the Office of Emergency Preparedness, for example, showing that given the need to conserve national fuel supplies, currently expected growth in automobile use would be "unacceptable"—are persuasive.* American autos and trucks each year burn 40 percent of all petroleum used in America, and one eighth of all petroleum used in the world. They are designed in such a way that they waste fuel. All recent auto changes, adding large engines, extra weight, extra options, particularly air conditioners, cause cars to use more fuel: the average mileage per gallon of an American passenger car fell from 15.3 in 1940 to 14.9 in 1950, 14.3 in 1960 and 13.7 in 1969. Auto selling wastes more resources, with cars designed to be scrapped quickly, and difficult to recycle, and with auto parts easily damaged and designed to be replaced instead of repaired. The market pressure to sell more cars creates a yet more wasteful use of the automobiles that people buy. The average car, this major national investment, is parked at least 22 hours a day. When it is used, it is likely to be more or less empty. Of the 82 percent of commuters who drive to work, two thirds drive alone, or 56 percent of all commuters: the efficiency of automobiles, in city streets, for moving passengers per gallon of fuel, is minute compared to the efficiency of buses, trains, taxis, or even jumbo jets, considerably less than that of the proposed SST, and little more than that of the old *Queen Mary* ocean

---

* The OEP study of energy conservation finds that the transportation sector of the U.S. economy is particularly wasteful and provides particular scope for conserving energy, but that the government has acted historically to "aggravate the energy problems" because "it favors development of [air and] highway transport."

liner. Such waste is in no way coincidental to present automotive arrangements—arrangements which also misuse, with reckless profligacy, national and personal wealth and the human energies of millions of people, including, perhaps, the auto production workers of whom Henry Ford wrote that "in our industries, we think of time as human energy [yet] wasted time does not litter the floor like wasted material."

Such costs, and such waste, are not trivial relative to national development. People will continue most evidently to waste money and resources and energy; the question will be, rather, whether auto civilization is what people want to waste their chances on. Automotive arrangements are not absolute, or absolutely appealing, but depend on a particular conjuncture of social and historical partiality—a conjuncture which has had the most serious national costs. As the social partiality which supported auto expansion erodes, it will become possible to see auto transport as one way among many, a particularly costly way, of spending and wasting resources.

The adjustments required to pay the costs of past auto partiality will be both expensive and disruptive. The political struggles now developing over antipollution legislation, government regulation of the auto industry, distribution of highway revenues, are certain to intensify. One senator has described the possibility of "extremely emotional" conflict. The auto business will face ever new troubles as national resources are rearranged. Past coalitions of political support will disintegrate—the interests of auto makers, oil corporations, highway lobbyists, auto rental firms, components suppliers need no longer correspond, as different corporations attempt different modes of diversification. Foreign auto expansion may damage U.S. employment. The economic costs of auto stagnation will be severe, for areas of the United States, and for hundreds of thousands of American workers whose jobs, already intensively reorganized, may be reduced, or moved, or destroyed.

American overinvestment in automobiles and in highway transportation involved perhaps the largest commitment of resources in the history of any country. Yet a reduction of the automotive system is possible—because the reasons for auto growth are historical, and contingent, and no longer compelling, and because, at least in large American cities, the auto system no longer works. The habitual inertia of auto investment, in highways and jobs and the shapes of cities, is as gigantic at least as the inertia of nineteenth-century railroad investment, but like that earlier repudiated investment, auto investments can be transformed, grassed over, used again.

The decline of auto-industrial domination does not mean the decline of American business, and the transformation of auto investment will not require the abandonment of transportation, or of highways, or of American automobiles. Economic distortion made possible automotive power, and makes necessary its reorganization: it seems within the grasp of social ingenuity over some decades to preserve the benefits of auto freedom without present and perceived excesses of automotive waste. Many of the great advantages of rail investment were lost in the convulsions of twentieth-century business evolution, but automotive benefits could be saved—by improving vehicles, traffic patterns, the utilization of autos and trucks, by changing modes of transport, from autos and trucks to trains and new transit systems, by reducing the total demand for transportation.

Some changes will occur quite easily as auto domination contracts. I would expect, for example, that automobiles should in the future be used more for leisure and pleasure, and less for daily routines: more improved recreational vehicles, and fewer commuter cars. Close to half of all auto trips involve driving to and from work, or going shopping, functions in which automobiles confer much frustration and social cost, and comparatively little enjoyment, and which could be performed relatively easily by more or less elaborate public-transit systems. Improved bus services, or a city car-rental scheme, could be used for commuting to work (and work would be created in newer transport industries). The most modest rearrangements could improve ways of shopping, reducing the need for second family cars; even in existing suburbs and shopping centers, for example, dialed buses could transport shoppers, if markets and groups of stores across the country provided efficient, free delivery vans, which could also be slow, nonpolluting, and used busily all day.

Beyond such simple readjustments, improvements in transportation should be expected from the development of research and technology—as the struggles of perpetual business evolution yield some progress, some new products. These improvements might also be directed to replacing the routine functions of auto travel—either by mass transportation, or by replacing such travel altogether. Some of the more trivial and tedious reasons for travel could be removed, by improved communications or telecommunications. More generally, it seems likely that different social changes will affect the total demand for transportation. If fewer people work in large factories, and more people work for the government or in small service offices, jobs may become more decentralized. If fewer people have children, the demand for suburban life may fall. More people may live near their work; people may live in what the OEP calls "clusters," or in neighborhoods.

American arrangements for the end of auto domination will require social and economic adjustments, like other adjustments in world history—adjustments of peculiar force, which yet remain a part of continuing national change and repudiation. Automotive dominance was a consequence of business evolution even in the days when Henry Ford built his new factories, and Alfred Sloan looked down at the "splash of jewel-like color presented by every parking lot," and it is industrially mortal today as it faces decline.

Notes and Acknowledgments

(These notes mention only major sources and references)

All the statements in this book by company executives are quoted from public or published sources, except in the context of two meetings described in chapters 5 and 7.

I would like to thank the people I talked with at Lordstown, Ohio, on several occasions since March 1970.

Parts of this book appeared in different form in the *New York Review of Books,* and I am grateful to Robert Silvers. I would also like to thank Kate Mortimer and Mary Kaldor, Jason Epstein, and Alexander Cockburn.

Chapter 1.

Sources used in Chapter 1 and throughout this book include: Alfred Sloan's *My Years with General Motors* (New York, 1965), Henry Ford's *My Life and Work* (Garden City, 1923) and *Today and Tomorrow* (Garden City, 1926), the *Statistical Abstract of the United States,* for several years, and the U.S. Department of Labor *Handbook of Labor Statistics,* for several years. Other constant sources include the annual reports of corporations, the *Wall Street Journal, Automotive News, Fortune,* and *Motor Trend.*

Richard Gerstenberg's remarks, page 3, were quoted in the *Wall*

Street Journal for December 7, 1971; James Roche's, page 4, in *Automotive News* for December 20, 1971, and in the *Wall Street Journal,* March 26, 1971; Roche's, on page 7, in the *Wall Street Journal,* March 30, 1971; and Edward Cole's, page 14, in *Fortune,* January 1972. Lee Iacocca's statement, page 6, was quoted in *The New York Times,* February 16, 1973. The Office of Economic Preparedness study mentioned on page 10 is *The Potential for Energy Conservation,* published in October 1972. The government study mentioned on page 14 is *The U.S. in a Changing World Economy,* published in April 1972. Henry Ford II's remarks, page 18, were made in a speech given on May 31, 1972. *The Road and the Car in American Life* (Cambridge, 1971), page 19, is by John Rae. Giovanni Agnelli's speech, page 20, was given on October 26, 1971, to the Society of Motor Manufacturers and Traders, in London.

Chapter 2.

This chapter uses the U.S. government's *Historical Statistics of the United States, Fortune's* directories, the *Automotive News* Almanacs, *Ward's* Automotive Yearbooks, Frederick Taylor's *Principles of Scientific Management* (New York, 1947), and *Ford: The Times, the Man, the Company* and *Ford: Expansion and Challenge* (New York, 1954 and 1957), by Allan Nevins and F. E. Hill.

Company testimony, pages 28 and 32, was given at Price Commission Hearings in Washington, D.C., on September 12–14, 1972. Figures about Detroit in the Depression, page 36, are taken from *Detroit* (New York, 1972), by B. J. Widick. Statistics about industrial productivity in the 1960's, pages 29 and 40, were published in the U.S. Department of Labor *Monthly Labor Review* for August 1972.

Chapter 3.

Information about the Vega comes from, among other sources, company speeches, company advertisements, and published road tests. I am also grateful to Judith Lesser of the Center for Auto Safety in Washington, D.C., and to my Vega-owning friend, Sophia S.

J. Z. DeLorean discussed the Vega in a speech given at the New York International Auto Show on April 3, 1970, in an article in *Motor Trend,* August 1970, and as quoted in *Automotive News* for August 17, 1970, and September 21, 1970. His remarks about Chevrolet submarines, page 57, were quoted in the *Wall Street*

Journal, May 26, 1971, and about automotive quality, page 90, in *The New York Times,* November 18, 1972. The GM Assembly Division executive, Mr. Joseph Godfrey, pages 62 and 90, was quoted in the *Chicago Daily News,* May, 16, 1972. The senior Ford executive, page 62, Mr. Robert Stevenson, was interviewed in *Autocar,* August 13, 1970. John Brooks, pages 69 and 70, wrote about the Edsel in *Business Adventures* (New York, 1969). The study of suicide, pages 74 and 75, was described in *The New York Times,* September 18, 1972. Federal Trade Commission complaints, pages 76 and 77, were reported in the *Wall Street Journal,* October 13, 1972, and December 6, 1971. The Center for Auto Safety, pages 76 and 85, wrote to Mr. Gerstenberg on September 1, 1972. *Fortune*'s profile of an auto dealer, page 78, was published in December 1972. The Jung experiments, page 81, were described in *The Automobile Industry since 1945* (Cambridge, 1971), by Lawrence White. Vega recalls, pages 85, 86, 88, and 89, were described in letters to Vega owners, and in the *Wall Street Journal,* May 9, May 15, and July 5, 1972. Ralph Nader, pages 87 and 88, wrote about the Corvair in *Unsafe at Any Speed* (New York, 1966).

Chapter 4.

GM's labor relations executive, Mr. George Morris, page 102 and later (pages 120 to 123 in Chapter 5), was speaking on September 22, 1972, at the Flint, Michigan, Rotary Club. His speech was sent to me by GM's public relations department. *Fortune,* page 106, discussed factory automation in July 1971. The president of the Lordstown local union, page 108, was interviewed by Agis Salpukas in *The New York Times,* January 23, 1972. The Chevrolet coordinator, page 108, and other GM executives, page 111, described Lordstown in *Automotive News,* August 10, 1970. Joseph Godfrey, pages 110 and 118, was interviewed in the *Chicago Daily News.* May 16, 1972, and in *Automotive News,* October 4, 1971. The examples of "management tough-mindedness" mentioned on pages 115 and 116 were described to me by Lordstown workers in the summer of 1972. Edmund Wilson, page 116, and quoting Samuel Marquis, page 115, wrote about Ford in *Detroit Motors,* published in *The American Earthquake* (New York, 1971).

Chapter 5.

Sources for this chapter include: the Shelley Report, *Climbing the Job Ladder,* published by the American Foundation for Automation and Employment (New York, 1970); *The Anachronistic Factory,* an address given by D. T. N. Williamson to the British Royal Society, March 16, 1972; *Alienation and Freedom* (Chicago, 1964), by Robert Blauner; "The Treatment of Disability," by R. A. Sokolov, *Journal of Occupational Medicine,* February 1967. I am also grateful to Neal Herrick, and to Irving Bluestone of the United Auto Workers.

The GM "position paper," page 125, was quoted in the *Wall Street Journal* and *The New York Times,* July 22, 1970. The industrial sociologist, page 126, is Robert Blauner, in *Alienation and Freedom,* mentioned above. J. Z. DeLorean described his early career, page 128, in an interview with Karl Ludvigsen in *Signature,* November 1972. Marx's observations, page 130, are from "Machinery and Modern Industry," in *Capital,* Vol. I (New York, 1967). The Department of Labor study, or "Working Conditions Survey," pages 133 and 134, was described by Neal Herrick and Robert Quinn in the *Monthly Labor Review,* April 1971. "The Anachronistic Factory," pages 142 and 143, by Wickam Skinner, was published in the *Harvard Business Review.* January 1971. Thomas Fitzgerald, page 143, and pages 150 and 161–164, wrote "Why Motivation Theory Doesn't Work," in the *Harvard Business Review,* July 1971. James Roche, page 151, was interviewed in *The Wall Street Journal,* December 6, 1971. Lee Iacocca, page 151, was interviewed by William Serrin in *The New York Times,* July 18, 1971. Joseph Godfrey, pages 151 and 152, and, earlier, pages 133 and 144, was interviewed in *The New York Times,* April 16, 1972, in the *Chicago Daily News,* May 16, 1972, and in *Automotive News,* October 4, 1971, and April 10, 1972. Agnelli's remark, page 156, was quoted by Anthony Sampson in *Vision,* May 1972. My meeting with the GM personnel executives, pages 158 to 161, took place at the GM Building in Detroit, on October 27, 1972. Chrysler's executive, page 165, was interviewed in *The Wall Street Journal,* December 7, 1972. Leonard Woodcock, page 166, was quoted in *Newsweek,* March 23, 1973.

Chapter 6.

Books used in this chapter include: E. J. Hobsbawm, *Industry and Empire* (London, 1968); Jane Jacobs, *The Economy of Cities* (New York, 1969); Thorstein Veblen, *Imperial Germany and the Industrial Revolution* (New York, 1964); Samuel Smiles, *Lives of the Engineers* (London, 1879); and *British Historical Statistics* (London, 1972), compiled by Mitchell and Deane.

Pininfarina, page 169, wrote about Detroit in *Nato Con L'Auto-mobile* (Milan, 1968). *Life*'s issue on Detroit, pages 169 to 171, was published on October 23, 1939. Sources for the decline of British industries include *The First Industrial Nation* (London, 1969), by Peter Mathias, and *The Development of British Industry and Foreign Competition, 1875–1914*, edited by D. H. Aldcroft (Toronto, 1968). The British "National Efficiency" Movement, pages 177 to 180, is described in *The Quest for National Efficiency* (California, 1971), by G. R. Searle. *Made in Germany* (London, 1896), pages 177 to 179, is by Ernest Edwin Williams. Gramsci's essay, page 180, is reprinted in his *Prison Notebooks* (London, 1971). John Brooks describes the 1920's boom, page 182, in *Once in Golconda* (London, 1969). Engels' observation, page 183, is from *The Condition of the Working Class in England* (Stanford, 1968). Early British attitudes to the automobile, page 186, are described in *The Motor Car and Politics* (London, 1971), by William Plowden. Engels' essay, page 190, is quoted in his 1892 preface to *The Condition of the Working Class in England*, as above.

Chapter 7.

Former Secretary Peterson, pages 194 to 195, wrote to *The Wall Street Journal* on December 11, 1972, and classified American industries in *The U.S. in a Changing World Economy* (U.S. Government, April 1972). Joseph Godfrey, page 196, was interviewed in *Automotive News*, April 3, 1972. The *Business Week* survey of productivity, page 198, was published on September 9, 1972. *Fortune* described productivity, page 199, in February 1972. Edward Cole's remarks, page 201, were quoted in *Automotive News*, March 4, 1972. Doctors and auto mechanics, page 203, were counted by the U.S. Census Bureau, *International Herald Tribune*, October 23, 1972. The Main Battle Tank, page 204, was described in *The Wall Street Journal*, March 27, 1972. Winnebago Industries, page 205, suffered a serious decline in 1972 and 1973, both in business prosperity and in stock-market performance; competing RV corporations continued to expand. Chevrolet's RV festival, page 206, was described in *Automotive News*, April 12, 1971, and GM's motor home, page 207, in *Automotive News*, November 20, 1972. The average occupancy of automobiles, page 207, and the use of auto energy, pages 211 and 212, is described in *The Potential for Energy Conservation*, mentioned earlier in the notes to Chapter 1. I visited William Spreitzer, pages 210 to 211, on September 19, 1972, at the GM Technical Center in Warren, Michigan. Mini-Cars Inc.'s experiments, page 215, are described in *Motor Trend*, July 1971. The average driving speed in New York City, pages 215 to 216, is shown in the State of New York's *Air Quality Implementation Plan*, April 1973.

Chapter 8.

Sources for this chapter include: the *Transportation Sector Working Paper*, published by the World Bank, January 1972; the *United Nations Statistical Yearbook* for several years; *Japan: the Government/Business Relationship* (Department of Commerce, June 1972); *The Japanese Motor Industry* (United Kingdom Stationery Office, 1972); the London *Financial Times*; and the *Far East Economic Review*.

E. M. Estes, page 222, described world automobile production in *Automotive News*, March 1, 1971. Giovanni Agnelli discussed auto booms, page 224, in his London speech mentioned earlier in the notes to Chapter 1. The Datsun Cedric, page 227, is described in *The Japanese Motor Industry*, mentioned above. The Kennedy Hearings, page 228, of the Senate Labor Subcommittee on Worker Alienation, took place on July 25–26, 1972. Matsushita, page 233, was described in *Fortune*, December 1972. Ford's plans for Spanish expansion, page 234 to 235, were described in the London *Financial Times*, December 12 and December 30, 1972. Prospects for investment in South Vietnam, page 236, were described in the *Wall Street Journal*, January 19, 1972. The French employers' report, page 237, is quoted by Michel Bosquet in *Le Nouvel Observateur*, Paris, March 20, 1972. Milton Friedman's opinions, page 237, were described in *Fortune* for August 1971. Asian automotive destruction, pages 241 to 242, was described in the *Far East Economic Review*, notably on December 16, 1971, and February 22, 1972.

Chapter 9.

Automotive commuting, page 247, and energy consumption, page 249, is described in *The Potential for Energy Conservation*, mentioned earlier in the notes to chapters 1 and 7. The gas line mileage of passenger cars, page 249, is shown in the *Statistical Abstract of the United States*, 1971

Index

ABOUT THE AUTHOR

EMMA ROTHSCHILD, born in London in 1948, received her B.A. degree from Oxford University in 1967, and then did graduate study at Massachusetts Institute of Technology. She worked for *The London Sunday Times* as a reporter/ researcher in New York City. Her articles have been published in *The New York Review of Books, The Listener,* and other magazines.